Love,
Mom

Love

HYPERION
• • • • •
New York

Poignant, Goofy,
Brilliant Messages
from Home

Mom

DOREE SHAFRIR
AND JESSICA GROSE

Creators of PostcardsFromYoMomma.com

Library of Congress Cataloging-in-Publication Data

Love, mom : poignant, goofy, brilliant messages from home /
[edited by] Doree Shafrir and Jessica Grose.
    p. cm.
  ISBN 978-1-4013-2342-4
  1. Mothers—Humor.   2. Love, Maternal—Humor.   I. Shafrir,
Doree.   II. Grose, Jessica.
  PN6231.M68L68 2009
  306.874'30207—dc22

2008052945

Hyperion books are available for special promotions and
premiums. For details contact the HarperCollins Special Markets
Department in the New York office at 212-207-7528,
fax 212-207-7222, or email spsales@harpercollins.com.

Design by Nicola Ferguson

FIRST EDITION

1 3 5 7 9 10 8 6 4 2

For our moms,

Roberta Steinberg and Judith Ebenstein

CONTENTS

Contents

Contents

Contents

Contents

Contents

ACKNOWLEDGMENTS

The authors would like to thank Gretchen Young and Elizabeth Sabo at Hyperion, for getting the project from day one; Kate Lee and Larissa Silva at ICM and Elisabeth Weed at Weed Literary, for shepherding us through this process; Brad Walsh, a great photographer; Lauren Le Vine, the best de facto research assistant; Pamela Peterson, for her publicity know-how; Eric Rachlin, who designed our website and patiently answered all our mom-ish tech questions; Christopher Silas Neal for illustrating our cover; Anne Schoknecht and Anna Knoell for designing our beautiful proposal; Alex Pareene at Gawker; Kerry Miller from Passive Aggressive Notes;

the Foggy Monocle boys, Jimmy Jung and Erik Dane; Lindsay Robertson and Gabe Delahaye, for letting us perform at Ritalin Readings; Diablo Cody, for being so supportive; and Sara Vilkomerson and everyone at Very Short List.

Doree would like to thank Marc Kushner, Niharika Desai, Jessica Pressler, Alex Balk, Choire Sicha, Emily Gould, her colleagues at the *New York Observer*, her brother Michael and her sister Karen, her dad, Avishai, for not being jealous that there wasn't a book about him, her mom, Roberta Steinberg, for being the inspiration for this whole crazy project, and most of all, Sam Cooper, for his support, love, and laughter.

Jessica would like to thank Anna Dever-Scanlon, Liz Stevenson, Lizzie Goodfriend, Mary Lydecker, David and Charlotte Winton, Anna Holmes and the rest of the Jezebels, her brother Jacob, her dad, Richard, for believing in the concept of blogging-as-career, her mom, Judith Ebenstein, for always having something smart and sassy to say, and Mike Winton, for always being there at the end of the longest days with warmth, kindness, and love.

And of course, the thousands of people who submitted their moms' emails—and the moms who took it all in stride, good-naturedly. Without them there would be no book.

Love,
Mom

INTRODUCTION

"I'm Just Being Your Mother"

I T ALL STARTED so innocently: a Gchat conversation in which we were discussing the emails our moms send us. "I'm sending you a hilarious email my mom just sent," typed Jessica, "because I think you will like it." "Ooh yay," Doree wrote back. "I love hilarious mom emails." After we shared a good laugh over the content of that email (which, to protect what little privacy Jessica's mom has left, we shall keep forever secret), Doree sent Jessica an email from *her* mom (the contents of which shall, alas, also remain private). "The one thing you need to know," Doree wrote, "is she's told me this story FIVE HUNDRED TIMES." "That makes it better!" Jessica responded. "My mom always tells me the same stories too."

A few minutes later, Jessica wrote: "Also our moms still both have AOL email addresses."

Then: "OMG," Doree typed. "OK. I just thought of a brilliant idea. We start a website called emailsfromourmoms.com and get people to send us emails from their moms."

"OMG THAT IS AMAZING," Jessica wrote back. "Let's do it."

We mulled over a few different names, and then Jessica suggested Postcards From Yo Momma. And thus a website, and a phenomenon, was born.

There was no way we could've anticipated the absolute deluge of emails we started getting as soon as the site went up. To get started, we sent out an email to a few of our friends, asking for submissions from their moms, and within twenty-four hours we had received over fifty emails from best buddies, distant acquaintances, and new fans. At that point we realized we might be onto a sort of essential mom-ness that wasn't just idiosyncratic to our own mothers—we had inadvertently stumbled on something that was universal in the modern mother-child relationship.

By the time Postcards was one week old, we had been interviewed by the largest newspaper in Canada, been blogged about from Australia to Texas, and had gotten hundreds of submissions from adult children everywhere eager to share their moms' particular brand of humor and wisdom with the rest of the world.

The floodgates had certainly been opened—but *why*? What was it about emails and texts and instant message conversations with moms that was so amusing and yet so touching? We turned to our own moms for some answers.

Jessica's mother, Judy, called dealing with her adult children a "constant negotiation." "You have this overwhelming love for your children, but you realize that as they get older, it's natural for them to pull away," she said. "So, as a mother you're always completely comfortable expressing the unconditional love, but your children sometimes need to distance themselves from it."

And email makes it easy for moms to express this love in a chatty, off-hand way. According to Judy, who is a shrink and prone to making grand sociological pronouncements, "Even though the subject matter of our exchanged emails is gossipy and very much about the moment, it is precisely this kind of ongoing interaction which is very important in maintaining a meaningful social network."

Doree's mom, Robby, also noted that there's definitely been a generational shift in terms of how parents communicate with their adult children. "When I was a college student, my parents would call on Sunday morning, and the conversation would go something like this: 'Hi. How's everything? Have a good week? Speak to you next Sunday.' Long distance was 'expensive,' and there was no chitchatting or calling at whim because we didn't have cell phones, and I had to be in the dorm room at a certain time," Robby said. "I'd certainly like to think I have more frequent and *meaningful* communication with my kids than my mother had."

These days, email, personal blogs, and cell phones allow moms to have an ongoing—even if sometimes one-way—conversation with their grown children 24/7, as if they were still living in the same home. When Jessica's mom emails her, she says it's "kind of like walking through the living room and seeing you sitting there. Something comes to my mind about what I need to tell you— something that's not important enough for a phone call, but I can get it right off my chest. If I really thought it was emotionally relevant, I would talk to you in person." And as Doree's mom pointed out, "When I email you or your brother or sister, I know the email will at least be glanced at. Since there's caller ID, you can choose not to take my call, but I—perhaps naively—believe that the email will be seen."

Technology also helps moms keep track of kids who are reluctant to be found. Intrepid moms who find that their kids have suddenly stopped responding to emails and phone calls can also turn to the Internet and find their kids' blogs, Facebook pages, and Twitter feeds. As Doree's mom told her, "I check your blog several times a day and *restrain* myself from posting comments. I did the same when your brother had one. I love it, and it really helps me feel that I'm keeping up with you." Likewise, Jessica's mom reads her blog daily. "I love seeing what you're thinking about," she said. "And that's what makes me feel very close to you. In a not particularly intrusive way, I can be part of your life."

When we started Postcards From Yo Momma, we worried—briefly—that our moms might think we were just mocking them, that they wouldn't grasp the site's subtext of sweetness and genuine affection. But we underestimated them. Not only did they totally get it, they continue to find it hilarious, and take solace in the fact that there are thousands—if not millions—of moms around the world who have very similar relationships with their adult children.

Since the launch, both our moms have been only slightly more self-conscious about what they've been emailing their kids. Jessica's mom said, "I'm more aware of making sure you know when things are confidential, but I don't care if you make fun of what

I'm writing. I'm just being myself. I'm just being *your mother*." And Doree's mom added, perhaps optimistically, "I do see that I email you guys less. Maybe we're talking more."

Besides, our mothers know deep in their hearts that they'll have the last laugh. One day in the not too distant future, we'll have similarly ungrateful children who will click open their in-boxes to find an email from us. They'll take one glance at our maternal missives and groan to themselves, oh *Mom*.

CHAPTER 1

"Your Blob Is So Funny and Clever"

BLOGS, IM SLANG, FACEBOOK, AND THE MYSTERIES OF THE COMPUTER

SINCE THE DAWN of time, mothers have seized upon the newest technology as a means of communicating with their children. Historians say that the first extant cave painting, depicting a lone bison, is around thirty-two thousand years old. We now know that this was a message from a mother to her son, asking him if he could teach her how to use the newfangled yoke that his father just bought.

Each day, mothers around the world are learning to harness the power of technology. They start with learning to turn on their various gadgets. Once they've gotten the confidence to master the basics, they're going to take baby steps into this brave new world. They'll be naturally curious and have a thousand questions, just like an actual baby. First come the Gchats. "Can you see me?" some mommas ask on Instant Messenger, fearing that the Internet is spying on them like an omnipresent big brother.

But it's really more like mom *is* that big brother. In the primitive olden days when mothers still pecked out missives on the type-writer and long before the Apple IIe made its clunky debut on the market, moms had barely any way to check up on their grown-up spawn. Nowadays, they're on Facebook, looking at their kids' pages and judging their friends. But it's really all over once they've found a child's blog—and a sign of the apocalypse if they've started their own. Soon they'll discover YouTube, and it's only a matter of time before videos of their beloved offspring, naked in the bathtub with a rubber duckie at age three, are plastered all over the World Wide Web.

* * *

My computer has software transmitted diseases (STDs) from all the software I had to download for a class and for doing assignments in another class. I hate computer STDs. ☹

I think my computer is more stable after I worked on it the day before yester-day but not as stable as before all the software downloads.

Computer with STDs

* * *

Hi Honey: Hope all is going well and you are not to stressed! Please take care and don't let all the traveling get to you. And Awards!! like OMG

Jennifer Gardner was on the Today Show today and talked about how wonderful the script was and how intelligent and nice you are. I hope you enjoy Minnesota, how about the weather it must be a shock to you after all the warm weather in LA. Where do you go after Minnesota?

I hope home for a few days so you can rest. (Do you notice I answer my own questions) ! I read the blog today and loved the article from the New Yorker, your blob is very funny and clever you have so much fun with it no wonder everyone Love's it. We are all well and looking forward to seeing again soon. The cat's are having a lot fun with this very large box, Larry has been in it and just looks out at you ...he is very..well you know ... crazy?

Have a great day and remember we are thinking of you

Love Mom

* * *

me: Mom, did you watch the Sex and the City trailer?
mom: Oh Hi, can you see me right now? No where is it?

me: hi! No, this is just instant messaging. I just sent the link to you, check your inbox

mom: ok, aren't you impressed with me on chat!!!!!!!!!

me: no, you are way too slow, stop typing and go watch the trailer

mom: Fine, is it goood?

me: SO GOOD

mom: How did you type that back so FAST!

me: Mom.

mom: OK I am going to go watch it now. bye bye

me: no don't go anywhere, just watch it and then tell me what you think

mom: ok
I CAN"T WAIT!!!!!!!!!WOW!!!!!YEAH!!!! when does it come out? It probably said, I am going to watch it again...

me: May 30th

mom: I better get moving, talk to you soon, Love Mom

me: get moving where? what do you have to do today? i'm the one who has to get back to my job, I have to go

mom: Work work work

me: you're ridic, lata playa

mom: Bye, Lata playa

me: Mom don't copy me

mom: Word

* * *

Mom

I feel so much more confident with the computer to the point that I don't refer to it as "stupid computer"' I think I am beginning to like it!!!!.

Un abrazo muy grande. LA MAMA

* * *

mom: I did not look at the web site yet. I can't do two things at once on this computer, I will check after we "hang up"
I have to go soon. It's movie day. We got screwed out of The Savages by a different release schedule due to V day. It's gone--replaced by The Spiderwick Chronicles

me: hmm

so is that what you're seeing?

mom: Actually, I better go. I want to look at that web site and I need to get dressed. PS I love you

me: haha ok thanks

mom: That's the movie not a closing!! HA

* * *

Sandra and I found out that one network has passed on our project and that bummed me out, but Sandra feels very confident about our web version getting funded. I may be on You Tube sooner than you think!

"Oh God", you'll say, "there's my aged mother prancing around on a hillside with a stupid wig on and carrying arrows..how humiliating!".

I say, "may we be so lucky!"

xoxo

Momo

* * *

mom: why does it say "hiding"

me: because i am hiding in a cubby in the library. that's my "away message"

mom: oh, you said it

I thought the computer-gmail did it

how would they know!

Oh, you don't have any more nazonex prescriptions, oh dear!

* * *

Please cleanup your facebook. Sex, drugs, lesbian stuff, no religion. People look at that before they hire you - Pres. Bush gets reports about this stuff, too. Listen to your mother — have a little common sense for goodness sake. Have some Christian values!

Your mother

* * *

My computer is back online. It had a virus.....gotten by using the Smiley faces, no less. GOOD GRIEF!! I told the computer guy that my sister uses them all the time, fer gawrsh sakes, and has for years. But I do it one time.............grrrrrrrrrrrrrr!!!!!!!!!!!!
Love you all!

* * *

Michael, I think you do too many drugs and say too many disparaging things about women on your blog. Love, Mom

* * *

my computer has the flu
no mail 'tween me and you
so here's a big hug
to cheer up your mug
and confirm that your mom est un fou *!!!

* french for "is a crazy person"

* * *

I know you both are probably joking around on your facebook pages, but.................... did you and Kate actually get married?
Love,
Mom

* * *

Hola hija querida, gracias por ser mi amiguita de facebook.
Yo aun no se como usar esta cosa, pero ahi ire aprendiendo.
so, see you around,
love you
Mom

Translation:

Hello my beloved daughter, thank you for being my friend on facebook. I still don't know yet how to work this thing, but there I will be learning.

So, see you around,

love you,

Mom

* * *

Hey Bob...thanks for ditching the condom picture on your blog...eeeew...not a nice thing to see.

I hop you & Elaine have a nice dinner. Love, MOM

* * *

Hi sweet pea!

how's that 40 degrees? I think the high in Montana is 12 and they have 12-18 inches of snow on the ground and it is supposed to snow every day until Sat.! I guess we'll see what it really is like in the winter! Any chance Dana Carvey will be there do you think? Actually if I see him I might make an exception and ask him is he wants to be my friend on facebook!

I love you!

Mommy

Love, Mom

* * *

mom: i just nailed the entire rock and roll section (british) on jeopardy
me: wow, nice!!!
mom: yeah!!! (me with the big L on my forehead)
i am playing with myself
ha
me: please dont ever write "i am playing with myself" to me
mom: thats why i did it

* * *

HELP!

The news is out! Dad bought me a Webkinz. It is reallly well designed and is the biggest craze I've seen in a long time.. It is comparable to the tamgachi and beani babies of your early youth. Every first grade through 5th grade student has one. They are awesome, yet a bit addicting.

I need your help. I can't make enough money to feed my Webkinz. I have failed at three jobs so far. Please do not check my resume. My Webkinz has survived on pudding which is the sale item.

Please tap into my account and do something about it. Remember, I can get kicked off the site if not used appropriately. No mating of Webkinz. Any ways here is the information you will need.

www.webkinz.com
username #######
password #######
Thanks, Gotta go and make some real money.
Love,
Mom
P.S. Don"t give my password away.........seriously

* * *

Joe,

I'd like to add you to my professional network on LinkedIn - this is Facebook for grown-ups.

-Mom

* * *

Love, Mom

i have no idea how to operate that I pod you have generously gifted to me. i cannot even get the thingie to turn on,
what am i doing wrong? i charge it and then nothing.
am i dumb or something/
HELP
Mom

* * *

I will e-mail you the chili recipe tonight. I am still thinking about whether you shall be allowed to come home, despite your many exclamation points.

On a different note, I heard a radio program today about Facebook, etc. and the speaker said that employers are looking at Facebook, etc. when they are making hiring decisions and that this can hurt you. Do you have a Facebook, My Space page? I hope not. It doesn't sound like a good idea.

 **ADVICE FOR MOMS**

PROBLEM: Your son, a junior in college, posts photos of himself on his blog, clutching a beer with his arms around several scantily clad women. He doesn't know you know he has a blog, but you are worried that this might be the reason he hasn't gotten any summer internships yet.

SOLUTION: *It's entirely possible that your son isn't getting internship offers because of the racy-ish content of his blog; after all, if it was easy enough for is <u>mother</u> to find, we can presumeh that it's popping up in recruiters' Google results as well. We know you're tempted to do something like leave a comment on one of his particularly scandalous posts, but try to contain that impulse—the more you publicly embarrass him, the less likely he is to take it down. But he's also unlikely to respond to scolding emails telling him about the evils of his website. Be gentle, yet firm in telling him to take down the photo; even when we've posted photos on public websites, sometimes we've managed to convince ourselves that our moms—or potential employers—just aren't, well, <u>smart</u> enough to find them. Don't be shy about proving him wrong!*

PROBLEM: At least once a week, something goes wrong with your computer, and you email one of your kids every time it happens. Usually they're quick to respond, but lately they've seemed less helpful.

SOLUTION: *Sometimes moms can seem to have a willful ignorance about learning new technology, and your kids are probably sick of getting multiple emails wondering where on earth your desktop trash can has run off to. (Just FYI, they've probably forwarded them to our website.) But now it's time for some tough love—from your kids. Besides, they might not want to reveal too much. Remember that saying about teaching a man to fish? Teach a mom to text, and it's all over.*

CHAPTER 2

"Love You All (Equally)"

SIBLING RIVALRY,
YOUR FATHER,
AND FAMILY MATTERS

MOMS DON'T HAVE favorites...right? Most would say they love all their children the same, but we know that's not *totally* true. Moms love each of their kids for different reasons—they may confide in their daughters, but their sons will always be momma's boys. Of course, moms use their kids to complain to about their siblings (especially when it comes to messy apartments and significant others), but they also really, *really* want their kids to be friends with each other. As Doree's mom always said, "Friends come and go, but you always have your siblings." (Cue eye roll...)

Dads, however, are another matter. In many emails, moms make their husbands out to be more like Homer Simpson than Cliff Huxtable—they invent weird things (like a makeshift hose dispenser with a bicycle wheel) and almost never cook dinner (if they do, it's microwaved). But moms also seem keenly aware that their relationship with their children is different than their husband's is—moms will often communicate messages from dads to their kids, usually along the lines of, "Your father wants to know why your cell phone bill was so high." Then there are the slightly awkward emails from moms who've gotten remarried, or have boyfriends. More than phone calls, email is a potent way of attempting to bridge the almost-inevitable misunderstandings and resentments that their adult children have toward the Man Who Is Not Their Dad.

But there's nothing like Aunt Miranda's inedible casserole or Cousin Larry's drinking problem to really get a mom fired up. Unless your family is the second coming of the Cleavers, getting together with them usually leads to one of two types of emails: Moms will either implore their kids to *please* just suck it up and come to Easter dinner (and *please* don't make fun of Grandma's floppy hat—you made her feel really bad last year!), or moms use email to commiserate with their kids about the inevitable nightmare that said Easter dinner will be. Families are, by and large, quirky and unpredictable and annoying and funny, loud and obnoxious and sweet and caring. What, you thought your mom came out of nowhere? (Oh, and also: They really, *really* want grandchildren. Couldn't you just make your mom happy for once?)

* * *

Heey girls

Can you believe that I can write to you both. Actually, your brother showed me. Last night we went to a tHAI RESTAURANT. iT WAS GOOD BUT NOT AS GOOD AS OURS. lAST NIGHT YOUR CRAZY ASS BROTHER WENT INTO TOWN TO STAY WITH TWO GIRLS FROM SCHOOL. tHE BUS RIDE WAS 45 MINUTES AND i CALLED HIM TO SEE IF HE WAS COMING BACK TO THE HOTEL BUT YOUR SLUTY BROTHER STAYED WITH THE GIRLS. gO aLEX! Pressed the Caps lock key didn"t feel like retyping. Today dad abd Alex are going white water rafting abd I will try and go et a back massage.

The weather today is lovely. Will call soon

Miss you and love you

MOM

* * *

mom: well I have to go. wish me luck--your sister and I might kill each other on this trip.

me: I'm sure it'll be fine

29

me: just be patient

mom: when you have kids you should stop at one. I wish I did.

me: Mom! you can't say that about her!

mom: it's good to know you're smiling.

* * *

Subject: What's up buttercup?

How are you? I hope you are happy and busy. I had 30 minutes of your sister's angst. If she contacts Adrian, you have my permission to beat the crap out of her.

* * *

dad and i gave up our seats for $400 vouchers, so now we're going back via orlando arriving at 9 PM. if anyone wants to call me i'm sitting in the airport..... love you all (equally) mom

* * *

Daddy is watching What Not to Wear now and is actually enjoying it. Maybe there is hope but I am not sure after the out fit today. I have to honestly say I have never seen him put together something that looked so bad. it could very well have been on 'queer eye'. It just amazes me that he doesn't see it.

"Love You All (Equally)"

Thank god he never went for a job interview in it.

* * *

Dear Children,

Tomorrow is Dad's 65th birthday - a biggie he is agonizing over.

You know how he is about birthdays. If you do nothing else, CALL HIM....preferably in the morning. PLEASE!!!!!!!

Love, Mom

* * *

I got an email from Daddy today. He said he has gas, but he doesn't think it has anything to do with the volcano. I told him to leave that in Argentina.

Love you!

Momz

* * *

Subject: RED ALERT

dad & i both got sick with diarrhea between 8 & 9 o'clock Thursday night --

don't know if it's the spaghetti we had for supper or what -- just warning you.

* * *

mom: Your Dad went to sleep at 8:30 last night. (sigh)

me: You're kidding!! Was he jet lagged?

mom: No. There was nothing good on TV.

me: Oh my. Is that a recurring thing?

mom: Who knows. I was out at a Social Action Committee meeting. Maybe he was hiding from Natalia.

* * *

'ood 'orning! Watching HGTV, doing computer stuff (bills, etc.), whitening my teeth, trying not to think about work.

Oh God – I hate when dad comes grocery shopping with me!! He complains about how expensive everything and wants to buy chicken gizzards.

* * *

I assume you know that your father got married a week or two ago. I figured that was what the insurance dropping was about. I just hope when he dies, you get his money and not the home wrecker. Love, Mom

* * *

your brother saw your dad yesterday am - drunk drunk but has his girlfriend's 2 month old kitten with him. wtf???? i made a crack about looking after her pussy - wrong wrong wrong I know! I am going to hell. ok, talk to you later.

* * *

*Subject: hi
i want grandchildren.*

* * *

File this away for VERY future reference in case you want to use family names:

Dad's grandma/grandpa names: Lillian and Sophie, and David Willard and George

Mom's grandma/grandpa names: Louise and Mary, and Frederick and James

* * *

i was laughing on the trip home - so much to think about after a family reunion... about us talking about getting professional photos done- but really, we don't have that kind of family where you all dress in a white shirt and get family photos taken... plus betty would have had to take her oxy

tank out! i don't know why that made me laugh but we aren't that pretty of
family (well, some of us are!) i just can't take a photo!

* * *

mom: which one is he in the big picture

me: in the blue stripes

the really tall one

mom: he looks very bad and devilish! was he drunk?

me: are you serious? we were drinking but not drunk…yet

mom: I mean he looks really cute and kind of resembles Daddy did
when I met him! HAHAHA

me: i know! he reminds me SOOOO much of dad. its weird. he's like a
man.

mom: okay yeah he's a real man, looks nice and smiley, I like his grin.

is he going to be bald?

how are his legs? Sounds like we are talking about the merits of a horse!

Please don't tell him though, it would be so creepy

* * *

Can you believe that Henry & Jill (one of his daughters) are coming through
here on the 17th of this month and Dad started the conversation by telling

them how "great" he is doing now and of course, they just must spend the night. They always have been the biggest free loaders and this means I have to give up my bed, my bathroom, worry about feeding them and then change the sheets, etc. again after they leave. In addition, have to clean the porch furniture now, instead of waiting until a little closer to time for you all to come. Dad said he just cannot understand why the sheets would have to be changed. He said I am "stingy, mean, hateful, etc." That I had my friends stay here before and he did not complain, I told him that for one thing, I am the one who cleans behind my friends, in this and in every case, I am the one to do it all. Oh, well, even Annie, as good as she was always called me just in a frenzy when these free loaders came and left her house. They brought all their kids and she fed them, slept on the couch, etc. Also, these Smith's have done this to us at least five or six times during the years.

Call me if you get a minute. Right now I need you to either tell me I am crazy or reassure me or something.

Mom

* * *

Ur Dads Gettin old He Didnt Even Notice The 2 Girls Hangin From Theos Mirrow He Must Only Have Eyes For Me

CHAPTER 3

"I Had Never Heard of a Dental Dam Before"

SEX, LOVE,
AND RELATIONSHIP
ADVICE

LTHOUGH MOST OF us would like to think we were the products of an Immaculate Conception, the sad truth is that most of our mothers have had sex. In fact, many of them are still getting it on, perhaps even as you read this! Since they've been through it themselves, mothers love nothing more than to add their two cents about your significant other—or marked lack thereof.

As usual, safety is a big concern among mommas with fornicating children. Most kids probably cringe at the thought of discussing STDs with their mom, but that doesn't stop her from sending them articles about the HPV vaccine on a semi-regular basis. And even if she thinks her child's new paramour is clean, Mom will definitely need to weigh in on his or her future earning potential and/or attractiveness.

But most of all, moms just want their offspring to be happy. In fact, some of them attempt to take their children's romantic fate into their own hands. Whether it's setting up an online dating profile or meeting prospective sons-in-law at the pub, moms are just trying to help.

* * *

It was great to see you today. I'm really happy for you that you met someone nice. Here are Mom's three rules for a new relationship (the three "N"s):

Don't nag
Don't be needy
Don't be neurotic

Guys of all ages just flip out over these things(probably because it reminds them of their mothers.) I have recent experience! It's not anti-feminist, just a fact of life. I am not trying to scare you. Be cool!

Love,

Mom

* * *

You do realize that cold sores on lips are generally an outbreak of herpes right? Don't get all grossed out. Almost every single, individual has been exposed to herpes but make sure you know your partners. Yeah, I know I'm grossing you out even talking about this. You shouldn't be kissing anyone while you have it just in case. There's stuff at the drugstore you can get which is for cold sores. Also, if you think it might just be from chapped lips, you can try some Vaseline.

* * *

Subject: Unconditional Love

It's hard-wired into parents, part of our DNA. We love our children, no matter what. I'm sure Paris Hilton's parents love their little skank - certainly Jeffrey Dahmer's mother loved him.

Dad told me about your conversation last evening. I'm sorry that you are feeling lonely. The life you've chosen (which I attribute to watching too much "Sex in the City") seems like a pretty lonely life. Friends are great but rarely do they work as a substitute for family or community. DC is a city of transients, at best, and everyone eventually moves on.

Fortunately, you are in a position to have lots of choices. You are not encumbered by a spouse or children and can decide exactly what you want in your life. My point is that some choices need to be made...make a plan while you have the resources and mobility to execute on it. If you aren't happy, do something about it. While I'm not going to elaborate on my own shortcomings and past mistakes, suffice it to say that you do have options and should think about them.

I love you,

Mom

* * *

This is the best article I have seen on the risks associated with oral sex and how to reduce them. I had never heard of a dental dam before. Please do read this.
Love,

Mom

* * *

we hope you enjoyed your weekend. well, because, we really enjoyed your visit. we were sorry to see jim ill, but so pleased that he seemed more at ease so that he felt more free to speak. he is such a good, kind, sensitive, upright, principaled person. he is indeed a keeper.

love
mom

* * *

How is your boyfriend doing? He should talk to someone. Maybe be proactive?

* * *

mom: Is it because you lost your manpower?

me: No, Mom if that was it then we would still be married. Listen I'm not ready to tell. When I am ready I'll tell you.

mom: Is it because you go with men?

me: What?

mom: Do you go with men?

me: What makes you think that?

mom: It is natural for some men to go with men. If that is what it is then I want you to know that I will still love you. No, I won't still love you. I will love you even more.

me: Yes, Mom that is it.

mom: I knew it. I knew since you were five years old.

Your sister knows, too. She said you would get beat up in school. And your Dad knows.

me: I wish someone had told me.

* * *

Subject: Man With HIV Jailed For Knowingly Infecting Woman
This is to warn you and your friends to keep your panties on this
Weekend...
Love, Mom, R.N.

* * *

Once again, my dating history is such that I didn't really even like the guy
(I do remember that much but can picture his face; he had curly hair, kinda
afro like); so no groping inside the costume; I probably smacked his hand
every few moments. I certainly kissed a few toads before I met your Daddy.
Another funny story to cheer you. I dated this guy named Roger Wilson, and
he wore glasses; I didn't really like him too much either and def. didn't want
to make out. Anyway, I knew when he was getting ready to plan some on me
as he always took off his glasses.

Love,
Mommy

* * *

I think that you want reassurance that someone will care about you the way
you need them to. You just met G so give him a chance to see what he is like.

"I Had Never Heard of a Dental Dam Before"

He does not want you to think that he has lost his mind over you, he is taking time and going at an acceptable pace so that he won't overwhelm you. He is calling and asking you out, at this stage that is what he is supposed to do, you go to parties with other people and that has nothing to do with how you feel about him, right? Remember you with ASSdrew when he met you, he may think you are dating other people. Just slow down, take some breathes and look at the bright side. Love, Mom.

* * *

look, he thought of you. he may have already committed to the Preakness and became confused. look, the guy deserves to go and do. it doesn't mean he "doesn't like you" = it just means he's not consumed with you because he knows he will be seeing a lot of you. he's normal. you aren't. relax. You don't need to be so urgent. pretty soon they'll put a siren on you and you'll be an ambulance!!!

your trot down crazy road has started.

* * *

good news!

Our insurance covers: THE HPV VACCINATION.

but, this is NOT a license to have wild, unprotected sex, y'know!! hehehhe-hehee.

xox,
ema

* * *

Honey,

So glad you like the boots! I enjoyed hanging out with you too - let's do it more often!

Mmm, three boys - pace yourself, baby!

Love you!
m.

* * *

I am a little confused... what might Jessica have told Dave? So Dave really does like you in a girlfriend way? Mom

CHAPTER 4

"I Saw an Engagement Announcement for Dan"

MOM
THE WEDDING
PLANNER

MOMS HAVE ALWAYS lived for the day when they can plan their kids' weddings—and, thanks to email, they can become rather vocal when they think that their kids are taking too long to tie the knot. These messages tend to escalate from gentle hints (often in the form of relaying that an acquaintance of the same age has gotten married) to not-so-gentle hints (registry suggestions when there isn't an engagement on the horizon) to, finally, overt pleading.

But once moms are satisfied that their daughters and sons are marrying someone worthy, they throw themselves into it whole hog. After all, email has only made it easier for moms to constantly barrage their kids with suggestions on everything from party favors to the first dance. And once their kids *do* get married, there's always room for a joke or two about the husband or wife they've chosen.

Of course, when moms are discussing someone *else's* wedding, all bets are off. Anything and everything is up for critique: the flowers, the DJ, the location, the bride's dress, the best man's speech, and, especially, the food. Implicit in the criticism of other people's weddings is the idea that any wedding planned by *them* would be a thousand times better.

* * *

Input on an idea: Just stopped in at the Yummy store at the Kittery Outlets and the gummy frogs with the marshmallow bottoms caught my eye. They are green and white. Large bags of them are only $2.99. My first thought was this is our color! Price is very good! And, the thought came to me that the magnet on the refrigerator says you have to kiss many frogs before you find a prince. See where I am going with this?

Maybe we could find pretty white bags and tie green string around the neck and decorate with the stamps I bought yesterday. Your input would be warmly received.

Your adorable Mother,

Me

* * *

Ok - the video - I think we can do 2 - we will need a video for after the wedding or we will replay a video - but we will need time to move flowers and for Bill to take a few pictures - I am ok with Tracy doing a video for a few reasons - one - she really wants to help out - it is something she can do - and we need a mom freindly video - nothing embaressing - but my family wants to see what Tim looked like as a little boy - Tracy says he did not have blonde hair - which I would have thought he did with his brothers—my family wants to remember what Trish looked like as a little girl and vice versa for Tim's family - it is a time of love and remembering—nothing embaressing at all - but tasteful - WE will have time before the weddign to play 2 videos - or dv's - then after teh wedding we can play yours again

we received one pair of the girls shoes and they are perfect - the extra ribbon has been shipped - I think all is well - and on time for the wedding - love you - will talk to you later - we won't know anything about Livi till May - when we go back

* * *

I saw Mary this week, she said that she thinks Ben and Jenny will end up getting married. She said that Jenny gave Ben an ultimatum, he moves out of his parents basement by March or they are through.

I cant eat those Fiber One bars except when I am absolutley not leaving the house. So I have a ton of them. I'd like to take them in my lunch to work but they have proven to be too deadly.

Love, mom.

P.S. I went shopping today and bought you a grey sweater dress/sweater to wear with leggings for 10 bucks.

* * *

what is the edicate for day following the wedding? should we invite out of towners over for food and drink? and to see your place I and dad would do it. like a open house type of thing? veggie trays, cheese trays, snacks, pizza dip!!!!!! I don't know start at 11am. that way people, who are early risers can get up have breakfast relax come over for a visit before heading home!! let me know so I can plan!!!

by the way do you like tiffany lighting? I have found the perfect torch light, stain glass is red yellow and white with carved wood twist poll., very delicate, stunning I could see it with your living room dinning room. your brother wants to give you something special for wedding gift. let me know today.

go to "_theshoppingchannel.ca_" - item # 609135," the allistar" pls. respond ASAP

Peace MUM

* * *

a service for 8 is $366.00, and sur la table is having a going out of business sale and everything is 20% off. this would be an unbelievable bargain for less than 300 dollars, i would even get a service for 12, for an everyday, meat set, _if i was putting together a truso for someone_. its quite a find. sure a better purchase than spending on a cashmere dress or something. i wish i had the extra money that i could just buy stuff and put it away for the future.
love you.
Mom

* * *

hi honey;
I was waiting your phone call last night - didn't you say you will call me back after 9;30pm--
anyhow, I love to send you flower or something for your engagement to

congratulate but thinking time is too long maybe bus is left already???
love,
mom

* * *

My poor sweetheart.

I encourage with all my heart... but I tell you what I always tell you- he is who he is and he tells you who he is everyday.

Your love should make him want to be better- but it probably is already clear to you whether or not that is possible.

So then the question remains

Can you stand it the way it is?

He pushed you into this very fast...

You said when you first starting dating that you would know by the summer if it was going to work.

The engagement ring doesn't change that.

Give it your best shot darling.

Let me know if I can help.

One more thing - I know I said that the fact that it's hard makes it valuable.. but I'm not sure about that.

Maybe when its right its easy—

* * *

FYI: I also saw an engagement announcement for Dan Meyer. He is living in FL near grandma. Wasn't he on the cross country team?

MOM

* * *

HA! With your luck the recesive gene you carry from me may mate with a nothing gene from casey and Voila===your child is a morning person and hence YOU become one out of necessity!

love

mom

hee hee hee!

* * *

Wanted to let you know this is " She Murders Weekend" on Lifetime. Tell your husband I'm thinking of him. Luv Mom

 **TOP 10 REASONS . . .**

Top 10 Excuses for Why Kids Haven't Called Their Moms

1. "I don't get cell phone reception in my apartment."
2. "I was over my minutes this month."
3. "I don't listen to my voice mail; I didn't know it was urgent."
4. "My phone was off."
5. "No missed calls came up."
6. "I couldn't find my phone."
7. "I forgot to pay my bill so my phone got shut off."
8. "My phone fell into the toilet/washing machine/sink/swimming pool/ocean."
9. "I'm trying to minimize my time on the phone because I'm afraid of getting brain cancer."
10. "I sent you an email!"

Top 10 Reasons Moms Are Worried or Upset That Their Kids Haven't Called

1. "Someone could have hacked into your email account and impersonated you—I want to hear your voice."

2. "The last time we spoke you said something about away for the weekend and I haven't heard from you since then."
3. "I heard there was salmonella/E.coli found in eggs/lettuce/tomatoes/meat sold within a fifty-mile radius of your apartment."
4. "I called you four times yesterday."
5. "I haven't spoken to you since you went out with that guy you met on the Internet."
6. "I spoke to your brother and he said you talked to him yesterday, but when I called you didn't answer."
7. "Your Facebook status update has said Life's a party!!!! since Friday."
8. "I got a text message from you but I deleted it by mistake before I read it, and I thought maybe you were trapped in a car trunk somewhere."
9. "I know your phone hasn't been disconnected, because I just paid your bill."
10. "There's something *really* important I need to talk to you about. Could you please call me?"

CHAPTER 5

"What's Your
Take on
White Jeans?"

GIFTS,
SHOPPING ADVICE,
AND HOW TO USE EBAY

MANY PEOPLE HAVE fond memories of watching their mothers get dolled up: sitting at their mom's vanity, watching with awe while their mom chose a gleaming new outfit from the closet and fixed her hair into artfully shellacked buns. But even moms who were stylish in their youth can suddenly find themselves woefully behind the fashion times. Low-slung jeans seem to be a particular point of confusion among the baby boomer set.

Oddly, even though moms will turn to their kids for fashion advice, they're still full of commentary about their kids' stylistic choices. Moms have a wealth of knowledge about undergarments in particular, and have even gone so far as to do extensive bra research online. They're always willing to go out and purchase frilly underthings for their daughters, and for some reason moms love buying boxer shorts for their adult sons. We're not even going to hazard a guess as to what *that* means.

Moms aren't only fond of buying undergarments. Certain mothers love their trips to "Nordies," and the creation of eBay has been a godsend for moms who enjoy shopping as a competitive sport. Once they learn the eBay ropes (and usually their children have to teach them), they're buying everything from action figures to dresses and everything in between. It's an exciting new world of purchasing out there, and moms are ready and willing to tackle it.

* * *

me: John owes you $84 in ebay so far....if you want call him and tell him his payment schedule....maybe even half now and half next week? I may pay for half if I can as a gift

mom: I'm not too worried about a payment schedule since I have some leverage, I can hold Obi Wan Kenobi hostage.

* * *

got these 'mom' sneakers in all black (you can hardly see the alligator on the outside but it is visible......)also a cool pair of white leather pumas with black stripes and the big cat -what's your take on white jeans ......?? please advise

* * *

DO NOT GET SPANX. they stop circulation. It could cause fainting spells.
Really they are only for the very, very skinny who have nothing to push up
or down or around. Get something comfortable and not tight that will just
smoth you up and down.
Love the picture. thanks
I rsvp's to the Kick-off lol

* * *

yesterday I saw a calvin cline trench raincoat... it is shiny black pvc made list a
classic trench with a black cinch belt...it would be great for rainy days... it was
marked down from $ 300 to 50 and they has a small are you interested? it looks
like patent leather basically you just wipe it off. had a nice large collar.

* * *

Fwd: $4.50 flat-rate shipping on all bra purchases!
Hi M - In the interests of conserving(and healing) your back, would you like
to choose one of these bras for exercising? From some research I read a few
weeks ago, it is important to support the chest from the sides as well, which
is why the squashing sports bras do more harm than good. I have used 2 of
their bras for exercise in the past and they are excellent. Love Mum

Love, Mom

* * *

Carrie says you haven't shopped yet (ya, like when would you have had time). Just in case you're interested-- for dad I would suggest a non-plaid sports shirt (XL) and/or the book Hockey Night in Canada by the Numbers. I would like a black or dark red purse with a handle long enough to put over my shoulder.

See you hear for dinner next Saturday.
Da Mama

* * *

Oh my gosh--I am tickled that I got your taste just right. Yay. That brown is so yummy--like caramel. MMMMMM MMMMMMM.

I gave Nordies the right address, but the translation to the clerk at Nordie's was a bit dicey--not a bright penny, shall I say.

So glad they recognized the company name.

WaHoo for caramel shoes.

Love,

Mom

* * *

So I actually looked at ladies' golf clothes online and ick!

Don't dress like that. It's good that no other civilian ladies will be there – you can take liberties with the genre. I do stand by my ideas of yesterday, but ok, you could wear khaki pants and a sportier jacket if you want, and even a pull-over with a collar. Just avoid the pinks and greens, especially the plaid ones I just looked at. Lilly Pulitzer stuff is out – I never understood the attraction of that, even when Lilly was young (or alive, whatever). Love, Mom

* * *

I am the highest bidder. $75. thank you for your guidance for this difficult ebay procedure.
I have a meeting at 9 a.m. great to see you yesterday. tell your cat I'm sorry I missed her but I think of her often. LOVE your dyke hair!!!! and of course I love you.

su mama

* * *

i have a delicious day off today....b'day present to me from me......I am going outlet shopping....will be back late afternoon...if u r going home AFTER WORK

Love, Mom

BRING SOME FLIP FLOPS for your pedicure tomorrow...dad is working at home today so give him a call for pick up if I am not home yet....no cell phone yet!

Go Hookies!!! M

* * *

mom: I think I im'd myself - I thought I was sending you a message - ahhh - I don't think I am cut out for this method of communicating. :'(
me: haha

hi mom!
mom: Hi there - I sent you an message about going shoe shopping with dad tonight - did you get that one or am I the only one that read my message
me: no, i got that one :) but then it said you were signed off
mom: I seem to find myself all over the place - my learning curve is as big as my hips - and you know how big those are!!

* * *

Either you're just like me or I'm getting just like you... you know those brown pants that are too short. I always meant to turn the hem down but I always put them away without fixing them. Well I just took the hem down to get the initiative and I'm walking around that way. I just went down to the café and no one notice or said anything. They are actually the right length this way. I have to make a very small hem. I guess that I cut out too much... hope that you're doing well.. have a great day querida..... =)

* * *

Cool! I'll still hold out for the converse. They're completely transparent - you can really see the hand knit socks though them. I think all the other knitters bought them up though... they're a hot commodity. I might have to scout some out on ebay... AND Yes, thanks for reminding me. Is he starving?!! I should buy a few cans of wet cat food also and poor Hershey... Pepper's probably eating her dog food by now.

Is ashley home? I left my phone in the car. We already talked about her FAFSA. We're doing it tomorrow night. Or we can do it tonight when I get home from miles' registration. Tell her to calm down.

* * *

hey my darling daughter
enjoy your stay in new york also if u can manage to go tiffinay in ny u can

Love, Mom

go and brouse but if u want u can buy some thing for yourself there or in san francisco there is tiffay on post street on union sq san fransico. any way this is the product it is a teething ring but it is double teeting ring $125 prduct code 1837. see what u can buy too for your 21st as well there are tiffany strores everywhere in usa. have a great time there please be careful all the time - don't trust people too quicky but make friends.

love u lots mum x x x x x x

CHAPTER 6

"I Do
Actually Like
Your Hair!"

APPEARANCE

WHEN A FRIEND has gained weight, or gotten a bad haircut, or is wearing something trendy yet extremely unflattering (high-waisted pants, perhaps?), most people will politely keep silent, preferring to cast their judgments internally. It is universally acknowledged that moms are the only exception to this rule. In some ways, it's refreshing; who else is going to tell someone that their new dye job makes them look like a streetwalker, and they should really go back to brunette? On the other hand, sometimes moms can be a little *too* blunt, like the mom who not-so-subtly hinted over email that her daughter should get plastic surgery. That's one momma who should learn to keep her opinions to herself!

Still, all this consternation about what moms think of their kids' appearance does highlight one salient fact: They may deny it, but most kids really still *do* care about what Mom thinks about how they look, whether they're fifteen or forty-five.

Love, Mom

* * *

I so tired of not having time to be a girly-girl. I am getting my eyebrows waxed today, hair tomorrow. I may even go get my nails put back on, now that I have time for maintenance. I am gonna be "hot" for cabo. You young girls just better watch out.

* * *

I almost forgot to ask, did you get your hair cut? I think Rachel Ray found out about your idea to get a sassy new hair cut, because she cut her hair too? I not watching her anymore....'cause Nicole hates her.

* * *

No- you are not SCARY white.
Your makeup looks very nice, your dress is adorable.
Besides, ROYALTY IS white. That is why the queen always has someone carrying her umbrella.
Zayda just had MORE cancerous stuff cut out of his head by Dr. Shrager and Cynthia.

PUHLEEZE - STAY WHITE. I CAN'T TELL YOU HOW DAMAGING THE SUN IS - YOU

DON'T WANT TO KNOW.
Look at him, and, look at my sun freckles , which will prob. turn cancerous too.

* * *

Thanks for sending me the picture.....don't I look great! The photo shoot was grueling but I am quite pleased with the results XXXXX mom

* * *

Love it!, the neckline is perfect. Your shoulders will look killer in it. Very classy. But, here are my caveats, go and try it on. The gathers on the bottom of the boobs can, not always, but can, give the two potatoes in a sack look. The wide band on the waist can also give the dreaded dirndl effect and make the tummy jump out with a pooch just below where the band leaves off. Do you want the flowers just on the top of the band. I am afraid if we cover the whole band, it will make the waist look thick.

Tailored has always been the best look for you with that model's bone structure you have, and gathers usually an no-no. Even if you are a stick, gathers can plague you if the cut is too generous in the boobs and too *tight in the waist. But if none of these calamities befall you, then you have indeed found the perfect dress. I sound like Reese Witherspoon in Legally Blonde, lord!*

Love, Mommy

* * *

Your costume is absolutely authentic and you look smashing in it! I'm going to have it printed right away. Your pose is terrific, sort of the come hither look or the "come and see me sometime" look. Just great! You are sooo good looking!

Love, Mom

* * *

Got the pictures from Auntie. You and your apartment look great! Your kitchen and haircut are both terrific.
Love, mom

* * *

good morning! I left a message on the phone-somehow I forgot to put makeup on this morning! I put on moisturizer but not any cover up-any chance you could bring me some with a makeup sponge (under my sink)? I love you-I will leave the back door of the Sarah's classroom open so you can leave it on the desk if I'm not here! hugs and kisses!

* * *

Well, it does look well done, and it is a beautiful image. It is very large, however. As you know, I don't really get it....... But you're not me so let's just hope you still love it when you're 35—or they've figured out a cheap, painless way to remove tattoos.

Love you! Please don't get any more kittens or tattoos this year.

xoxoxo

Mom

* * *

Do you think I would look totally dorky without bangs? My forhead really wrinkles though...............let me know your thoughts.

CHAPTER 7

"We'll Go to the Urologist Together"

GETTING SICK,
GETTING BETTER,
AND FEAR OF
DENGUE FEVER

A S MUCH AS grown children like to push their mothers away, snarking and smirking over their moms' loving advice, the one time they're most willing to accept a mother's electronic touch is when they're in a weakened condition: sick in bed. And moms really step up their game when a child is ailing. They suggest all sorts of remedies—from tried and true ibuprofen and chicken soup to new-age, homeopathic antidotes like fish oil and "ions."

And that's just when a child is suffering from the common cold. Mothers can sometimes work themselves up into a frenzy about their children's well-being. More than one worries about the prospect of dengue fever, while others lay out excruciatingly detailed emergency medical kits that their children should have on them at all times.

But some moms go *completely* overboard when it comes to health and wellness. Some have taken to wearing surgical masks around the house to keep their husbands from getting sick, while others email random celebrities they see huffing and puffing on *The View* to suggest they see a physician. Even the most hypochondriacal, kooky momma's advice can help her babies get better; after all, laughter is the best medicine.

* * *

Hi. My colonoscopy was wonderful. Amazing drugs that put me out in the deepest sleep with a quick recovery. No polyps or abnormalities. I am good for another 10 years!
Good diet must help.

* * *

Honey,

Don't forget to wash behind your ears. You don't want that weird thing happening again.

As always, love mom

* * *

I got the yucky time, on the yucky day for the yucky appointment. We'll go to the urologist together. love mom

* * *

Hey,

Sorry I didn't call you back yesterday but I have been under the weather. I really feel like crap you know achy, a little temp, a little head stuffed, etc. So I have been going to bed when I get home. I just didn't want to miss my hair appt but I went to bed when I got home.

I'll talk to you when you come back. I printed out a map of Sawgrass anyway.

Love
Mom

* * *

did you have fun with Aunt M – what did you do. also if you plugged your light in did you feel the good ions coming at you and wake up happy. Just wondering. I thought if you used a mask you could put it by your bed and get ioned at night.

The place that sent it had lots of holistic things. Thymley solution - ever hear of them.

love you

mom

* * *

Sweetie! I have not had an anyeurism yet, but probably will before this sale is over. I bought a little demi-tasse and saucer for Granny, which I think is the same pattern as the ones in her living-room cabinet. I thought it was $1 but it turns out to be $40 - good thing I'm rich. If it doesn;t match hers I will be stuck with the stupid thing, and will have to buy that $4000 a pound coffee made out of civet shit to go in it. I can snort coke from the saucer... hey this is shaping up. Bring on the anyeurism!

I did think about malaria, typhoid and dengue fever when I first entertained the notion of the bump in Belize, but now I figure he/she will be nursing and not eating questionable food and swilling Mai-tais, and will be the only one not visiting tropical disease clinics when we get home. So yeah, LET'S GO!!!!!!!!

Gotta blow - sale - xoxoxoxoxoxox mamacita xoxoxoxoxox

"We'll Go to the Urologist Together"

* * *

me: I think I have strep

mom: I was wondering about that but I didn't want to jynx you

me: my throat is killing me

I can barely eat

which as you know is TORTURE for me

mom: ok you have to go to the student health services. You know if you have it or not

me: I know I do, but I don't know when I can

I have to set an appointment

and I work wed-sun

mom: well fuck a duck becky if you're sick you can't do anything!!!

me: well I have to go to work, marmoset

mom: well do you think they want to get strep

there are valid reasons to miss work

like contagious diseases

* * *

What are you doing getting bitten by mosquitoes?!! You will get MA-LARIA - and i will have to start worrying about that instead of typhoid.

Maybe you have got dengue fever even! Are the drugs working? Are you still alive?

* * *

I am having a minor nervous breakdown. Your Dad is going to stay home tomorrow and Friday, plus he will be there all weekend. This is my weekend off. He is the worst sick person. Whines and wants sympathy. Please help me. Your days in NOLA are numbered. I insist that Dad move to California with you. I will live here in peace with the dogs. This is the plan. Don't you like it?

Love,
Mom and Nurse (sort of)

* * *

Hi Craig,

Your list is incredible! My 3 kids have used it a lot and I just looked at it. I saw you on The View and think you are quite a guy! The reason I'm writing you is that you appeared to be short of breath. I'm a Jewish mother and felt compelled to tell you and suggest that you see a physician. I've seen too many sick people lately and don't want you to be one of them.

You have too much going on. (Pulmonary doc? Internist maybe first.) You don't have to respond. Just see a doc. I'll feel better.

Thanks,
Dana

* * *

You should see the barrage of germ fighting stuff I got at home. Been sleeping in another room, got N95 masks (those are the bird flu ones), brought home a can of Staph II (some hospital grade infection fighter we have at work), 1500 mg of C per day, and Airborne.

Ha ha ha ha.

* * *

mom: I'm sick fever

me: Oh no, I think there's something going around

mom: Going to Dr at 10 45 Called out my eyeballs are cold

me: Oh no

CHAPTER 8

"Did You Get a Waitressing Job at Hooters Yet?"

SCHOOL, WORK,
AND GROWING UP

THERE'S BEEN A lot of talk in the last few years about extended adolescence—the idea that even after going to (and in many cases graduating from) college, kids are slow to cut the cord keeping them tethered to Mom and Dad. The relationship between parents, especially moms, and their young adult children can be incredibly confusing. Kids want to be independent and have their moms leave them alone, especially when it comes to finding a job, or getting good grades, or meeting a nice boy or girl. But they also want their moms to meet them for lunch, take them shopping for dorm or apartment supplies, and (maybe most important) deposit money into their checking accounts. So who's to say it's unfair, exactly, for moms to be on their kids' case?

Well, moms *can* go too far. Sometimes they seem to lose sleep worrying about whether their kids have gotten their oil changed, and seem to check in every hour on the hour—via BlackBerry, text message, IM—to find out. Most of the time, though, moms are genuinely their kids' biggest fans, and what sometimes feels like nagging can also demonstrate to kids that their moms really care. Especially when an extra hundred dollars magically shows up in their bank account.

* * *

Hey on page one of the Post Dispatch business section today is an article that reassures me that the intership people you have been in contact with are not in the male sex slave business. I am sure you are greatly relieved:)
I'll bet you didn't know I knew how to make that little smily face.
Love
Mom

* * *

Subject: Spring is Here

love ya. Work hard at your job. It will come back to haunt you if you dont.
love mom

* * *

Subject: Re: Job Interview
OH MY GOD!!! YOU ARE A SUPER STAR *
* *Take
any day/time they ask you!!!
!!! love mom

* * *

I'd say ask for more, at least $20,000 or $25,000. You always work more hours
than originally planned. And by employing you only part time they are occu-
pying your life and making it impossible for you to have a full time job. and
harder to find an exactly matching part time job. Even if it's only two days
a week you still have to have clothes, haircuts, food, toiletries every day.
Where does this outfit get its money? Do they have reliable revenue stream
or is it a given that everyone who works for it will be subsidizing it to a degree
by working for less than market rate? In other words how much are the other
people getting paid? Are there any perks like free tickets to events you would
really like to go to? Is this a salary that comes with health care benefits and
unemployment insurance, or are you an independent contractor? Are you
getting paid by the hour or just one lump sum?

* * *

Not exactly accurate -- I said you'd be better off working P/T as a stripper as opposed to a hooker because you'd be turning away too many of the uglies out there -- although you would get your pick as you look cute in sweats!

* * *

Dad's had a very busy week working with one of the managers who came out to work some of his territory with him. Since they've been visiting facilities in the L.A. area, Dad's been getting up around 4:00 a.m. to head out there and doing most of the driving, arriving home around 6:00 p.m. after negotiating the crazy freeway traffic. He seems to be doing pretty well lately taking quotes for orders and does enjoy the job. Finally, a job he likes ! How ironic as we head toward the "Golden" years.

How's everything going with your jobs? Did you manage to find another one, or get a waitressing job at Hooters yet? I enjoyed our chat last week. Hope you're feeling more "up" and can see the light at the end of the tunnel, so to speak. These winter months are hard for us after the celebration of the holidays and putting up with inclement seasonal weather; sometimes it seems a long haul until spring.

* * *

Subject: New Job
Got my fingers, toes and eyelashes crossed. Do I have to keep them that way until Friday at 11? Actually with all the snow here, they may be frozen in position until then.
Love,
Mom

* * *

Subject: Things to Think About
I've been thinking about some things that need to be dealt with. I'm happy to help in any way you need it.

schedule carpet cleaning
schedule someone to come in and clean before you move in
activate utilities in new house
turn off utilities at apartment
turn in change of address at post office
hire movers
buy appliances and arrange delivery
order new checks

Love, Mom

insurance (homeowners)
taxes and insurance added to mortgage

*   *   *

Once you get to work today and find some LOVELY paper, why don't you print out 8-10 of your resume and just keep them in a folder, along with the list of references. That way you won't have to go through this running about, before an interview. Of course, there won't be any after this one, I understand, but just a thought. Of course, we didn't discuss but one is inflating their income too. Nothing less than presently making 50!

Was thinking about the suit also. Perhaps a camisole with just a bit of lace and/or straight across peeking through is the way to go. We should have grabbed one while in the lingerie dept at FB. I'm sure that you must have something though. Just slipped one on today while getting dressed and thought of it......

Chat later!

*   *   *

Thought I would bug you. #1- I received an envelope from G.U.; but it only contained the application for the food plan and the retail club acct. for the bookstore. There is no date as to when it has to be in, but I think we have some time for that. There has been no letters yet for tuition. #2- Thought I would let you know that Betsy Potter died yest. I'm sure you remember her husband Tim who came in twice a day. Apparently he has been taking the palliative care course and will probably continue to come in to help with feeding. #3- Have you heard any more about the apartment? Just wondering. I bought a big package of toilet paper for when you move. Wal-Mart had it on sale. 16 double rolls for $7.96. Very interesting, right? Oh well. That's all. love Mom

* * *

Hey daughter!

Go out there and enjoy your job, one day at a time. Enjoy the city and all it has to offer and remember that your life doesn't have to be a Sex and the City episode!

Make each moment count and try not to use the word 'suck' or drink a bottle of 'Riesling' (big calories) as long as you can!

Love, Mom

I hate that I have to read your diary and learn about our life in print with the rest of the world ....maybe you can call me sometime?

I love you and miss you and am soooo jealous.

* * *

This is your mother. I tried calling you but got your voice mail so I figure:

a) you were in a meeting astounding everyone with your ability to single handedly solve all work-related problems; or
b) .... you were in the bathroom.

Regardless, I love you!

* * *

I was wondering if you applied or considered applying as a "Mature Student". I think you meet the qualifications. You are over 23, have been out of school for more than 5 years, etc., etc, I believe the standards to get in are different than for those otherwise. Look it up - it is under their website, admissions, admission requirements, mature student. I know that is how a lot of people go back to school. Have a look at it and let me know what you think. FYI - I never thought you were lazy, quite the contrary. I don't know about the bus passes, but yeah, keep everything. We know that you are trying hard and it is only natural that we want you to be happy (in whatever you do). We just love you lots.

* * *

One last final...I hope it's all going well. I've been afraid to call because I didn't want to disturb you, but you're on my mind constantly. I love you. Call me when you're done.

Mom

CHAPTER 9

"Get With It!"

TAXES, CELL PHONE BILLS,
AND WHY MOM
WON'T SEND
THE FIFTH COPY
OF YOUR
BIRTH CERTIFICATE

A S WE MENTIONED in Chapter 8, there are many twenty- and thirty-somethings who are reluctant to leave the nest, known colloquially as adults who have "failed to launch." They enjoy the comfort of Mom's laundry, posh digs, and twenty-four-hour diner, otherwise known as her well-stocked refrigerator. Even after these youngsters are living on their own, moms still want to help out with some of the extras and never tire of reminding their sons and daughters to pay their taxes on time.

Not all mothers enjoy paying for their offspring's little extras, however. One mother admonishes her daughter about the myriad parking tickets getting sent to the parental household. "THESE TICKETS DON'T GET SMALLER OR GO AWAY—THEY ALMOST ALWAYS GET BIGGER AND MORE PROBLEMATIC!!" she e-screams. Some moms take a more passive-aggressive tact, giving very detailed instructions, followed by the phrase "Just a suggestion!"

The transition from extended adolescence to actual adulthood is often a rocky one, and generally moms just want to help—as long as helping doesn't mean paying their son's cell phone bill until he's eligible for Social Security.

* * *

Hey Kiddo,

How about we figure out about who pays for what on your cell phone? This month your total portion came to $35.35, what with a $7.64 download, the usual monthly minutes, $5 insurance, and $10 unlimited texting and such. Plus taxes, surcharges, and all the usual. That's not a small chunk of change anymore.

Not to make your life hard or anything but what say you start picking up these phone charges? Dad and I could actually drop down to 700 minutes and save more money, because you are actually the largest minutes user now that we have a landline that we use more and more. So we are keeping the minutes higher just for you.

What do you think makes sense now that you are out and earning well?

Let us know –

Mom

*   *   *

I got the info I needed. I could so steal your identity. I changed the password on your chase online account to the s..... one. The password that started with 'h' was my "maiden" name. Anyway, I made payments on both accounts, so by the 21st or 22nd you'll be under your credit limit.

I really love paying things off!! You know this means you can never put me in a nursing home, right?

Love,

Mother

*   *   *

Subject: New apartment

Ok, but I don't want the SS number to be a deal breaker or in some way cause [xxx] to have any second thoughts. If it comes up again, just say that your father was the victim of identity theft twice, when people took out credit cards using his personal information, and that kind of experience has caused your family to be cautious. Just don't come across as Polly Paranoia or Wilma Weirdo.

Love, MOM

* * *

The money I lent you (not leant) was not intended to be paid back. Just try and keep your bar bills down, which I don't think your father and I want to help you with. You've certainly helped me out countless times when I didn't have a pot to pee in, so I owe you.

* * *

Bet you thought they wouldn't find you, eh?? Well they found us, your parental units - got a notice to pay $150 by 10/18 or show up and protest the tickets. Dates are 7/20, 5/24, and 5/14, $50 each. So, unless you tell me different, I'm going to send in the payment right away, 'cause the Saturn doesn't want a new boot for Christmas, and (warning - parental advice coming: THESE

TICKETS DON'T GET SMALLER OR GO AWAY – THEY ALMOST ALWAYS GET BIGGER AND MORE PROBLEMATIC!!!)

Love you – let us know how the trip planning is going. Mom

* * *

Dear Bonnie,

It's Lola, your car, your mom noticed I was very dirty the last time she came to visit you at school and is sending you $20 in cash. Please don't use it on beer.

* * *

My dear son,

I wish I could count how many times I have sent you your birth certificate. You really need to develop a system to organize and preserve these important items. I'm not always going to be around to resupply you.

I am putting another original birth certificate and a copy of your Air Force birth certificate in the mail tomorrow. I do not have a copy of your SS card – but you DEFINITELY should have that card. Send for it TODAY!!

Love, Mom

This is the best I can do for you - it's YOUR responsibility!

Get with it -
I love you,
Mom

* * *

Haven't had time to be too bossy lately, but don't want you to think
I've completely given up that job of mine that I'm so good at!
Seriously, hope you're on top of this serious stuff -
1. Find and go to a dermatologist for a skin cancer screening
2. Get your driver's license
3. Register your car
4. Most importantly, don't for get that I love you!!!!!
22 days until your first holiday visit!!! Love, Mom

 **ADVICE FOR MOMS**

PROBLEM: You're still paying for your twenty-five-year-old daughter's cell phone, and last month her bill was a whopping $417.83 because she sent over seven thousand text messages. But she doesn't make very much money, so you feel like you should support her in any way you can. Besides, at least one hundred of the texts were to you.

SOLUTION: *It's easy: Stop paying your daughter's cell phone bill. You'll be shocked how quickly she manages to find a plan with unlimited texting!*

CHAPTER 10

"Now I Have an Excuse to Be a Beeatch"

GROWING OLD

I N THE PAST, moms probably went through menopause in private. Today, they're joking with their kids
about hot flashes and memory loss and hormone-
replacement therapy, and telling them about their group
excursions with the gals to see *Menopause the Musical*. Indeed,
these days, no topic is too embarrassing or graphic to discuss over
email, and yes, we refer here to colonoscopies.

There's a more serious side to all this humor, though. Moms
are genuinely concerned with what will happen to them when
they get too old to take care of themselves. Will their adult children have the means and the willingness to support them? And,
perhaps because they've seen *their* parents go through it, many
moms today make it abundantly clear to their kids that they don't
want to end up subsisting on Jell-O at the nursing home. As one
mom wrote worriedly, "Saw the Diving Bell and the Butterfly last
night with Belinda made me wonder what and who would pay for

long term care if one of us should end up drooling in a wheelchair for years."

Then again, some moms haven an entirely different attitude toward entering their golden years. Like the one who said this: "I'm relieved, at least as far as Stephanie is concerned, that I'm not totally branded as an old lady acting young. Next step—I wanna be a MILF."

* * *

Ellen is in the hospital and is quite sick. She just got out of ICU and had surgery for a bowel obstruction that required a colostomy--but thank God it turned out to be benign. Anyhoo, she's finally on the road to recovery, although she might end up in a nursing home for a short time to get PT. Daisy's been very worried. Brooklyn sounds great and I hope I can visit when the weather warms upa little. By the way, my old ladyitis is gone and the rheumatologisthas me on a very slow taper of prednisone, so hopefully I'll feel
normal for a long time. I never should have allowed myself to feel
that bad and depressed for that long, I feel like a new person now.
Can't wait to see you and hear your voice,
Love
MOM

* * *

Saw the Diving Bell and the Butterfly last night with Belinda made me wonder what and who would pay for long term care if one of us should end up drooling in a wheelchair for years... Your father's typical "push me off the cliff" answer wouldn't get me anywhere, other than jail... Then he said the firm would always have to pay him a wage... but as your father really is the firm, without him it would not do as well. Then, where would that leave us?
M

* * *

Christine says she doesn't recognize me anymore. I don't recognize myself. I can't stop fretting over houses and decorations and even LAMPS!!!! I actually looked at the new lamp last night and said to Christine, "Look at the lamp. Doesn't that lamp just make you happy looking at it?" This was after watching cable house hunting shows for 1/1/2 HOURS!!!

I've noticed this in older women all along... I always assumed they had empty lives and were filling it with lampshades. I now think it's the flip side of the teenage compulsion to live in messes. I suppose it has something to do with hormones and cave life- maybe the old cave women were the ones who kept out the diseases and germs.

Love, Mom

* * *

on my way out the door...going to the Gyn....checking out why I get these hot flushes and feel so tired. and crappy......going right down the doc list....tomorrow the gastro.... The L'chaim club has a speaker on love and sex....it was a riot....your father did not go....glad I went....learned a lot....lots of single old broads turning on to lesbianism...

and other interesting topics... it was fun.....waiting for your comments.... la de da......

* * *

FINALLY....IT IS OFFICIAL.....I AM IN THE TRANSITION STAGE TO MENOPAUSE. ISN'T THAT EXCITING?? Now I have an excuse to be a beaatch.

Due to all my symtoms as of late, the blood test does show elevated FSH which means I am moving on to my next stage of life. Not sure I am going to like it much.

Love

Me

* * *

I'm much older than my computer--are you suggesting that the older some-thing is, the more uselss it becomes? Because that's what I'm hearing (al-though I'm not hearing it very well.....)
Love,
your old mom

* * *

Hi, hope you had a good weekend and are getting ready for your holiday. Glad things seem to be better at work.

Freeeeezing here... now I know why old people move to Florida! Give me a trailer, some plastic flamingos, pedal-pushers, and some 'bodice-rippers' and I'm all set.

I need photos ... NOW.

Love, Mom

* * *

Thank you! I'm relieved, at least as far as Stephanie is concerned, that I'm not totally branded as an old lady acting young. Next step - I wanna be a MILF.

* * *

This is the latest should something happen to us: Go to a Jewish or mixed chapel, have a service for us, whatever size you want. Check my planner in my night stand for names of people to call. Have us cremated or if you prefer buried. Sit shiva at your house or ours or split it however you like. Do whatever is best for you. You can also choose to have a small service and a memorial service at a later date when it's more convenient for you. The shiva period is very healing so don't skip that. If you don't want the max time then do whatever you want. We'll edit this properly when we come home. Just don't want to leave you in a lurch.

There is no premonition!!

Much love,

Mom

* * *

How is your day going? You must be really busy. When I die, please don't put me in a safety deposit box, okay?

116

CELEBRITY MOMMA MAILS

Celebrities! They're just like us! They, too, have embarrassing mothers. Here are some contributions from the mommas of a few famous folks.

* * *

DIABLO CODY is the Academy Award—winning writer behind the 2007 smash hit *Juno*.

Hi Brookeeee!

Hope your trip back to LA was relaxing. We got in about 2 hours ago and I am happy to be home.. The herd of kittys are doing well, they missed us, Larry will not leave us alone (he keeps head butting me).

I read the blog (Postcards From Yo mother)...you all think your so so so funny!!! Well I have news for all of you...if all the mom's got together and started there own blob from their daughters do you what they would say....

thats right nothing!!!! because you guys never send us any emails....Ha Ha.. I thought that was very funny......

I love you, and everytime I see you when I go home I miss you more...

Love MOM

* * *

SARAH DUNN is the best-selling author of *The Big Love* and a new book, *Secrets to Happiness*.

subject: Monica

Looks like another false alarm. Webb asks us to pray she dilate soon. I sure hope so. They are both going crazy with the waiting.

Sorry we didn't get a chance to talk this morning. Kati had a bad morning with Nick and I was encouraging her to believe he will not end up hating all women because his mother yelled at him. If that were the case, Uncle Grady would have hated Nana and he adored her! Boys forget almost everything and girls almost nothing!!!!

I am playing Mahjong at 2:00 and then we are ordering pizza and watching "Dream Girls". Dad has an elder meeting. They will probably be late because they are considering the letter that is to be sent to the congregation regard-

ing the pastor's "misbehavior". It has been very interesting to watch all of that play out.

I expect you guys are really busy now with only 3 weeks until countdown time. Give a call when you get a chance but I realize you are going all the time with everything. I don't feel neglected.

Love, Mom

* * *

ADAM GREEN has released five solo albums and one as half of the Moldy Peaches.

Dear Adam,

I just flew in from Vegas. Boy are my arms tired! Ha

HAPPY BIRTHDAY - We got your passport so you will be able to go to Barcelona now

Look at supermediastore.com - I had no problems copying the dvd... try playing the dvd we made on the fujitsu computer.

Just wanted to caution you about what you eat in England. There is a disease you can get from eating beef there called "mad cow." Horse ok.

FYI, your music is being covered by reputable bands - Don't forget to sign up for efax.com. Its free and useful. You can get a free fax number, someone faxes to this and it comes to you as an E-mail which you can print out or look at.

Do you want to see a play in the village tomorrow night?

Also when does your road show begin? Can you get me the music videos before you leave. Cant get through to you on phone. Can you reply to this email. Shepler's jeans have arrived. Mom

* * *

WILL LEITCH is a contributing editor at *New York* magazine and the author of *God Save the Fan: How Preening Sportscasters, Athletes Who Speak in the Third Person, and the Occasional Convicted Quarterback Have Taken the Fun Out of Sports (And How We Can Get It Back)*.

Will: We need help in finding the best price for airlines (prefer nonstop) either STL or IND to LAS on june 12 and return june 21 from SFO to IND or STL. Also to rent a car on june 14 from LAS and return to SFO on june 21.

We know you get to live in new york so you are always on vacation but we old folks had to raise you and can finally afford to have one now that you are out of the house. So help us use the computer. You know how your dad hates it. Love You Mom

* * *

CHRISTIAN SIRIANO is the winner of *Project Runway 4* and a fashion designer.

Victoria Beckham has a brother named Christian. Can you believe it? The gods are with us!!!!

Love Mom

* * *

AISHA TYLER is an actress, comedian, and writer, and the former host of *Talk Soup*.

Well, I'm a timely e-mail reader! Much has come to pass since this missive. How was your trip? Having those kiddies in the car must have been an adventure. A little dry run for future parenthood!

I just want to say what a wonderful human being you are. So loving and generous in every way. Not to mention beautiful, talented, and brilliant! That's right! And I'm not just saying that 'cause I'm your MOM.

Your film sounds like it's going well. I can't wait to see what you've done. You are very brave. Now you have a car worthy of a producer and director; you can "style" as you drive down Sunset Blvd. Handsome young men can dash out to open your door and genuflect as you alight. Aaaah, what a fantasy.

I love you sweetie, and I'll talk to you soon. Smooches.

CHAPTER 11

"Hey, Nice Job
with Predicting
the Idol Winner !!!!!"

REALITY TV, POP CULTURE,
AND WHY MOMS LOVE NAPOLEON
DYNAMITE

THOUGH SOME MOMS might be technologically inept, almost all of them know how to turn on the TV, and many of them get wrapped up in the drama of *American Idol*. Whether they're ragging on the contestants or revering them, *Idol*-obsessed moms always have an opinion. But not all moms care about the Sanjayas and Carrie Underwoods of the world. One mom declares *The Hills* "beyond insipid" and thinks the Kardashian family is completely embarrassing.

That mom sounds pretty on the ball, but sometimes when mothers try to stay current, they fall a little short of total pop cultural literacy. Moms ask about that great new band Death Truck for Booty, and wonder if Two Pack is still releasing his rap albums.

When it comes to musicians and other celebrities, moms generally love the ones they grew up with. They follow Bruce Springsteen's political endorsements and reminisce about Princess Diana's untimely death. But the real thrill for moms is meeting their favorite stars. They freak out about meeting Rod Stewart and relay stories about seeing Johnny Cash. For years afterward, Mom will recount the time Aunt Edna was in line behind Ed McMahon at the In-N-Out burger in San Berdoo. Because if there's one thing that's equally universal as motherhood, it's the thrill of a celebrity encounter.

* * *

Tell me about the new Indigo Girls CD coming out on Tuesday. If I buy it will it be another mistake?

* * *

The concert was great, I actually enjoyed Josh Turner more than Carrie Underwood. Although, she was awesome. I wish you and Richard could have joined us!!!! I really don't think Jason was into too much. He wanted to scalp his ticket before the concert. I guess when you like groups like Tool and metal head crap, Carrie Underwood seems a tad tame.

Love you,

Mom

* * *

That reality TV kills me. I would love to hear more about the project your friend is doing. That Soup Talk has a field day with something called "The Hills". Their conversations are beyond insipid. Are you familiar? It is like eavesdropping on several 8 year olds. At least if they were 8 they would still be cute, but people like the Kardashians are so embarrassing. I think the writers strike was definitely a factor in helping this genre to survive. I just remembered something else, tell your friend. Probably over 40 years ago Public Television aired a program about a family in California named "Loud". Seriously. They agreed to have cameras 24 / 7 in their house! There was a mother and father and 4 or 5 children (mostly teen-agers). Eventually the wife handed the husband divorce papers (ON CAMERA) and had an affair with one of the technicians or something. Their oldest boy was on all sorts of meds for hyper-activity and eventually when he came out of the closet and moved to NYC I think they gave him a spin off show or something. Anyhoo, it was a hoot. It was the only reality TV back then. I remember thinking is was dumb, but PBS showed it for quite a while. Tell your friend to check it out. Nobody copied the idea again until very recently, I think. American Idol is reported on the news every morning as if it were a stock market statistic.

Gotta run.

Love ya

Love, Mom

* * *

HEY, NICE JOB WITH PREDICTING THE IDOL WINNER !!!!! WHAT A FANTASTIC SEASON. I WAS JUST REVIEWING THE SHOW LAST NIGHT ON THE INTERNET. WHY DON'T YOU AND ELEANOR VENTURE OUT TO HOLLYWOOD AND MEET SOME NICE, INTERESTING GUYS??? I'D LIKE YOU TO DATE DAVID COOK',,, OKAY,OKAY. LUV, MUMXXXOOOOO

* * *

If marrying/being the domestic partner of Napoleon Dynamite meant that I'd have to like tots-n-cheese, I'd do it. I love them.

* * *

Yes the guy with the dred-locks is Jason and the kid with the purple highlights is the Sanjaya knock off. Everyone hates him.

* * *

mom: I can't talk; I'm watching the Diana documentary on that Tender Loving Care channel.

me: Do you mean The Learning Channel?

* * *

Have you been watching the Gabriel Byrne tv series about therapy. he is really a STUPID therapist, but the acting is good. he missed an erotic transference that one could sense after about 2 minutes. then he didn't know what to do with it.

love
mom

* * *

94.9 predicts that Seyesha goes home.

and get off David Archuletta's back. He sounded fantastic. He has had a tough week with all the bashing of his dad. what happen to David Cook? First time I actually liked him.....and first time his appearance didn't make him look like he hadn't bathed in weeks. (greasy) He actually looked good.

* * *

me: hey i got your text what's up?
mom: did u pick up my wee yet?!!

* * *

Went to Walk the line. Real good movie. Did I ever tell you my uncle Ed (Becky's dad) Gave Johnny Cash a lift once in Rochester. Yup, Him and his geetar. I weigh in tonight, so I'm trying to be reeal good today. It's 0 degrees outside. And I'm not going out until I have to. Dad and I went to a play at College of Mousetrap. Kids did good, fun, job. Leta mea tella youa don'ta tippy toea arounda mea anymorea. One guy was Italian. Love Mom

* * *

me: I think my professor is divorced, but who could divorce such a sweet, little man?

mom: You know what they say, don't you? "When they got home at night their fat and psychopathic wives would thrash them within inches of their lives."

me: My mom just quoted Pink Floyd.

mom: Yep.

* * *

Tired tonight... we had the final big night of the convention. It was the Rod Stewart concert and was really good! We were amoung the group that was able to get a photo with him before the concert... pretty cool. He wasn't as chatty as Colin Powell was, but nice. He rocks really well and you forget how old he is.

Have you given a call to Grandma and Grandpa yet?
love,
Mom XXOOxo

* * *

mom: I only have three things left on the wall of work.

me: wooo!

mom: And only one of those has not been started.

The other two are nearly done.

And one of them is to watch a movie.

me: wow

mom: So that on the last day of class we can talk about "Pam's Laby-rinth" as if it were not a sexual thing but a deeply moving, socially sig-nificant, Latina magical realism thing....

Christ....

me: well, it is called Pan, not Pam

so at least the title isn't quite so creepily sexual

mom: Pan? No shit? The instructor keeps calling it Pam.

me: hahahha

it's Pan's Labyrinth

mom: Maybe that's the Spanish translation.

Love, Mom

* * *

me: bruce springsteen just endorsed obama

mom: well shoot - now I guess I have to change my ringtone and get rid of all my albums!

me: i'll let you off the hook this time.

though i am a bit disappointed in him

mom: sorry - I told him Hillary was the way to go!

he never listens...

* * *

Subject: Fossilized Feces Tell Tale of Earliest Americans, NPR

This is some important SHIT!

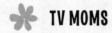 **TV MOMS**

The following mothers are television's most notable, beamed into millions of houses for years—with syndication, sometimes decades. Even when these kooky characters are at their most outlandish or evil, most viewers can find just a hint of dear old Mom in them. And even if these fictional females are nothing like one's matriarch, they certainly are entertaining.

Marge Simpson, The Simpsons
Though this beleaguered blue-haired mom is merely a cartoon, the size of her heart is superhuman. In nearly twenty years of weekly hijinks, Marge has survived nervous breakdowns, accidental boob jobs, a failed pretzel business, and thousands more minor indignities. Even with a husband like Homer and an ungrateful whelp of a child like Bart, Marge manages to stay positive, warm, and above all, loving through every trial and tribulation—and all without mussing a hair in that beautiful beehive.

Elyse Keaton, **Family Ties**

Meredith Baxter-Birney made working motherhood look easy and adorable as Elyse Keaton, Ohio architect and mother of four. Elyse and her husband, public-radio employee Steven, were ex-hippies turned bohemian bourgeois who managed to spawn a young Republican and a Valley Girl while still keeping their cool. Elyse deserves a special prize for not ripping off her son Alex's bowties or stealing his monogrammed briefcase at his most annoying moments.

Lorelai Gilmore, **Gilmore Girls**

Who says moms can't be BFFs with their daughters? Lorelai, who gave birth to daughter Rory when she was sixteen, was more like a cool older sister than a mom. She spewed pop culture references a mile a minute and even went on double dates with Rory without her daughter spontaneously combusting from embarrassment. Moms like to use this show as guilt-trip material to try to get their daughters to call home more, as Lorelai and Rory never quite cut the cord.

Clair Huxtable, **The Cosby Show**

Sure, Cliff Huxtable as played by Bill Cosby was the ostensible star of *The Cosby Show*, but everybody knows that the real heart of the series was Clair. She worked days as an attorney and still managed to find time to deal with the shenanigans of her five kids. Fear of the patented Clair Huxtable look-of-death (pursed lips, arched eyebrows) certainly kept Sondra, Denise, Theo, Vanessa, and Rudy from getting into too much trouble.

Laura Petrie, **The Dick Van Dyke Show**

Those Capri pants! Those pearly whites! That adorably fifties flip! Mary Tyler Moore was the archetype of fifties motherhood as Laura Petrie, dutiful wife and suburban mom. She might not have been the most liberated lady in the land, but MTM is the only woman in television history who could make crying look cute.

Lucille Bluth, **Arrested Development**

Martini-swilling, money-embezzling, and insult-hurling, no one would mistake Bluth family matriarch Lucille for Mother of the Year. Despite the fact that her husband, a construction baron, went to jail on fraud charges, Lucille continued to spend the barely existent family fortune, all the while demoralizing her mostly ne'er-do-well children. Sample barb, concerning daughter Lindsay: "Oh, she thinks I'm too critical. That's another fault of hers." Zing!

Roseanne Conner, Roseanne

Like Lucille Bluth, Rosie was another momma who did not mince words. You always knew where you stood with Roseanne, a hard-working, no-nonsense broad who was mom to four kids. Rose-anne kept it real, showing a warts-and-all version of American motherhood, where she and husband Dan had to try hard just to make ends meet. Even though Rosie had a sharp tongue, she was a big softie underneath it all.

Ann Romano, One Day at a Time

One of the first single moms to grace the boob tube, Ann Romano showed that you don't need a nuclear family to make motherhood work. She and her two daughters moved to Indianapolis, where Ann found work as an ad exec. Ann managed to take care of both her teens during the freewheeling, sexually adventurous '70s and work a fierce Dorothy Hamill 'do at the same time.

Kate McArdle and Allie Lowell, Kate and Allie

If Ann Romano paved the way for single motherhood on TV, Kate McArdle and Allie Lowell reinvented it. On the characters' eponymous show, they pooled their resources and their kids in one house after surviving a couple of messy divorces. Kate and Allie eventually started a catering business together, but the winning television formula fell apart when Allie got married and moved out of her cohabitational bliss with Kate.

Murphy Brown, Murphy Brown

Murphy Brown wins the prize for being the most controversial TV mom in history, as then–Vice President Dan Quayle publicly denounced her during the run-up to the 1992 presidential election for choosing to become a single mother. In the series, Brown gets the last laugh: She dumps a truckload of potatoes on Quayle's front lawn, prompting a fictional DJ to joke that the VP should be glad he didn't publicly misspell "fertilizer."

CHAPTER 12

"Here Is That Recipe You Wanted"

FOOD AND MAKING MOM'S SECRET ARTICHOKE DIP

THERE ARE FEW things a momma is prouder of than her recipes, and she's always touched when one of her kids requests her super-secret method of making chicken soup. But what used to be passed down via recipe cards or dog-eared cookbooks can now be done via email, and most moms also take this opportunity to let their children know that any variation on their sacred cheese puffs as put forth by Rachael Ray or Martha Stewart will turn out vastly inferior. Moms are particularly proud when their kids are planning a party and request a favorite dish from their childhood; as one mom wrote to her son, "Here is the Taco salad recipe. It is always a big hit. BUT mix RIGHT before serving since the DORITOS will get soggy. Everyone loves this."

Of course, also mixed in with the ingredients is the acknowledgment that most moms are still a little ambivalent about their kids growing up. Trips to Costco will usually prompt moms to ask their kids if they can pick up a twelve-pack of ravioli for them; underneath it all is the concern that without them, their kids would be eating ramen noodles every night. It works both ways, though. Moms will often ask their culinarily inclined kids for cooking suggestions, and expect an instant response regarding how to best cook chicken breasts.

Naturally, some moms are adamant that their kids keep their best recipes a secret. One mom warned her children: "This recipe is one of the family recipes, like the old-fashioned sugar cream pie, that can never be revealed to anyone else. Sorry but it is a rule. We will have to kill you if you divulge it and trust me, it will be an ugly death . . ." We *think* she was joking, but then again, her daughter didn't include the recipe—proof that a momma's wrath is still feared.

* * *

Just talked to Bobbie and we have "a plan". She would like us to come to her house about 2:00 She will serve drinks/beer/wine/soda. We'll put out some food:

Layered bean dip

Hickory farms sausage/cheese

Sliced turkey breast

Fresh fruit bowl

Birthday cake - carrot cake - I'm going to get the sheet cake from Costco - it is way too much but it will freeze and we both like it and it would be Linda's flavor choice

I'll also get some flowers there to put on the table. We will use paper plates and napkins. I'll put the scratch offs on the "tree" and that will be her "gift". We already sent her cards on her actual birthday, so I won't do another card. Linda sent her a couple gifts then too and I sent her a gift card to Applebee's on Mother's Day and she has already used it once for lunch for herself and Pat xxxxx.

Sound good?

* * *

Dearest Peepers:
This recipe is one of the family recipes, like the old-fashioned sugar cream pie, that can never be revealed to anyone else. Sorry but it is a rule. We will

143

have to kill you if you divulge it and trust me, it will be an ugly death... Now on to the recipe.......

Good luck. Please destroy this recipe once you have memorized it. I love you.
MOM

* * *

Subject: *Graham Cracker Cream Pie (attached)*
Here is the recipe I told you about. Would you forward this to Christina for me. Also, will you forward my new email address to me also, I can't seem to get back into the stupid thing.

Thanks,
Mom

* * *

If you need some food items I can get you cheaper, let me bring them to you. I plan on bringing some of my gluten free bread so I can eat break-fast at your place. Should I bring eggs? Jam? Juice? I have Indian sauces, rice dishes, and soup. With a little chicken breast we could have an Indian meal one night. Or just cook some of your Basmati rice for the rice dish. Other ideas?

* * *

I can't figure out to manipulate the cursor to write the recipe for the brownies so the cocoa is 1-1/4 cups and the flour is 1-1/4 cups so add that to the recipe and try again and don't blame me you brat , love Mom

* * *

You told me to give Sue my recipe. NEVER! NEVER! NEVER! It is the only thing I make well and therefore will never share that recipe. It still makes me feel good that Coach even mentioned it in his speech at the end-of-season banquet.

* * *

DO YOU HAVE A METHOD FOR DRUMSTICKS THAT YOU CLEAN SO YOU DON'T GET THAT BLOOD SEEPING OUT WHEN THEIR COOKED . THAT DRIVES ME CRAZY AND I THOUGHT IT WAS YOU .

MOM

* * *

What does one do with a wedge of blue cheese?

Mom

Love, Mom

* * *

Hi angel!

We bought everything you requested at Costco this morning!

And for tomorrow's dinner menu we have:

Veal Cannelloni and Rainbow (colors of pasta) Cheese Tortellini

Dessert will include Nuns' Farts!

See you domani.

Ciao bella!

Mommers!

* * *

Do you think Jessica would mind sharing her ham with cola recipe with me? We are having ham for Easter, and the way she was talking, it sounded like her recipe was a really good one. If she says OK, please email it to me.
Love ya,
Mom xoxo

* * *

I am pretty sure I told you that I bought a Calphalon Grill pan (nonstick) a few weeks ago but I had not used it yet...

Well, I tried it out tonight. I have really missed having grilled hamburgers since I moved here sans bbq grill, so for my first use of the new grill pan I grilled 2 lbs of ground beef shaped into 8 patties. The result was great...only thing missing from these burgers was the charcoal/outdoor flavor one gets from cooking on a charcoal grill outside....

The pans ridges lift the meat up enough to drain the fat from the burgers as they are cooking. The process takes place in the kitchen with no problems from inclement weather, flying insects, or fire blazing out of control which requires a lot of water to get back under control...

And lastly the nonstick coating is damned easy to clean! So all in all, this grill pan beats a charcoal grill on every point! Get one!

* * *

I'm taking a poll.. ok its only the two of you, so i'll be the tie-breaker - ha.

For c'mas dinner (sunday) should we have

a) a sit-down meal (not ham or anything that boring, i'll do it up)
b) soups and sammies and favorite goodies

No cheatin by talking to each other!
mama.

* * *

Wow - I just saw the pix pf the shish-kebobs. They really look yum-o as Ra-chael Ray says. That is one of my favorite meals (next to spaghetti). I love the shish-kebobs with rice. Yum-o.

* * *

Subject: My boss is very sweet
You wont believe what Valerie did for me. She was going to make a chicken gumbo soup, so she went to store 1 (1st visit) and bought kosher chicken. as she was driving home she realized that the recipe also called for chicken broth and that would probably need to be kosher also, so she drove back to the same store for the broth (a fair assumption since they had the kosher chicken). Store 1 (2nd visit) did not have the kosher broth. she went to store 2 and found kosher chicken broth in the box.......all was going well

until she told me that she sautéed the vegetables in ....
BUTTER!

I am so touched that she went to so much trouble. how about that?

* * *

Could you send me the recipe for the Amish bread? Or just call; if I'm not here you can just give it to me on the message tape. Get all better!
Thanks, Mom

* * *

Hi Honey...great talking to you earlier...I miss our little chats Here is that reipe you wanted.

ARTICHOKE DIP.....USE 9X9 PAN

1 SMALL JAR MARINATED ARTICHOCKS, DRAINED, CHOPPED

1-8 OZ. PKG. CREAM CHEESE

1/2 CUP MAYONAISE

1 C. PARMASAN CHEESE

SEASON TO TASTE...GARLIC SALT, RED PEPPER, ITALIAN SEASONING

SPREAD IN PAN, SPRINKLE WITH MORE PARMASAN CHEESE AND PAPRICKA

BAKE @ 350 UNTIL PUFFS UP, ABOUT 1/2 HOUR.

DIP WITH CRACKERS.
Mom

* * *

Hi Mark,

Here is the Taco salad recipe. It is always a big hit. BUT mix RIGHT before serving since the DORITOS will get soggy.

Everyone loves this.

I usually prepare everything and place into baggies and then mix right before serving. You will need a big bowl or I guess you could use a disposable tin foil large pan.

The last time I made it i did not have the green olives and it was still good. I think it needs the black olives.

Love,

Mom

XOXOXO

* * *

me: I'm trying to learn how to cook fish. I went to the farmer's market and got all kinds of fish.
mom: All kinds of fish?
Goldfish?

* * *

WOW!!! My sweetheart knows how to bake that is 10 times talented than her mom. Is it western culture that a perfect woman has to know how to baking and pressing the cloth? If does, you are qualified already.

Sure, e-mail me the recipe and I'm practice at home give dad to eat. I'm too cheap, am I? Love you and congratulation for the success on your baking.

Mom

CHAPTER 13

"I Would Like a Goat for Mother's Day"

RELIGION AND HOLIDAYS

HOLIDAYS ARE INCREDIBLY stressful for a mother. She has to contend with boorish Uncle Al getting drunk and making dirty jokes over the Thanksgiving turkey; she has to worry about her daughter's new tattooed boyfriend getting along with her prim mother-in-law over Christmas ham; she has to fret about running out of matzoh at the Passover seder. And that's only if her ungrateful children agree to come to the family festivities in the first place.

Kids often rebel against their mothers' religious instruction, and moms are quite reluctant to let their babies be eternally damned. And new-age moms are just as extreme in their spirituality. Some mothers celebrate the Spring Equinox by beating drums outdoors in the buff.

And then there is Mother's Day, the one day when Mom is supposed to sit back and let her kids do all the work—not that she doesn't have helpful hints about gifts and the celebration menu. Even on her special day, Mom always has her eye on what's *really* important.

* * *

I am sure you realize that I am quite upset with the fact that the 'new' so-called pope is in our country. The nerve!! He knows we don't want another pope - there is the one and only, yes, "Papal Babe". I am making protest posters and T-Shirts. Here's what I have so far...Just say Nope to Pope
Hey skinnny little german guy - the fancy clothes are way to big for you - get out wannabe!
Babeless in America
Pontiff go home!
Saint you ain't!
Popeless and proud
We don't need no stinkin popes.

* * *

Good morning moon unit. I saw a bit on the news last night that there is a group that celebrates the Spring Equinox all day by dancing and beating drums. What copy cats. I have already gone out side naked and have beaten my drum. I ran back inside when a man passing by went immediately blind.

I love you very much and I hope your day is divine.

* * *

Hello Children,

I need your wish list for Christmas. I want to start and finish my shopping on Thursday, my only day off.

If I don't receive your list by Wed night then I will assume you want nothing!

Merry Christmas!

Mom

* * *

Hi all, You know mothers day is coming up and I hope all of you can come and see me that day. You know I don't really need anything but I would like a goat for mother's day. If you want to you can each chip in 15 dollars and donate a goat in my name to Food for the poor a charity I really like. it would only cost a little and would mean a lot to me. Someone would have to organize it. This is just an idea - nobody has to do this. Nobody ever knows what to get me so I thought this would be a good thing - for Christmas you can get me another one.

love

mom

* * *

There seemed to be some discrempancy (sp) as to what date the first sedar is, so I called Temple Isreal. They said it is Saturday night. Lonny's son just called. He may come in for Passover, too. So what we may do is have Passover at his ex-wife's (we were invited) so we can both be with our kids. I want you to meet his kids anyway. What a GOOD OPPORTUNITY--IT WILL BE NICE IF THEY COME IN BECAUSE WHAT IS THE CHANCE THAT YOU WILL BE HERE AGAIN AT THE SAME TIme. (I hate when my computer changes to caps). I like a lot of people at a sedar anyway. It makes it a good one because you tend to do all the stuff and it would be cool for Katherine to see a real sedar.
I will let you kmow.

I love you!
Mom

* * *

OK, get a load of this. I've found a turkey farm called Mary's where I have reserved an organic 14 pound lady turkey for our dinner. You may not really care, but after I read Barbara Kingsolver's book about how turkeys are artificially inseminated and filled with hormones I decided to visit my local HEB grocery store and request ORGANIC and a turkey that has been able to enjoy the joys of S-E-X for at least a few months before the big slaughter.

We'll also have ham but that cannot be organic...at least according to the butcher I talked to about the fact that Butterball turkeys are bred so large they can't have S-E-X. He was polite and appropriate and said in his best Texas drawl...yes ma'm I did know that. He didn't even seem to be embarrassed and I figured, being a meat butcher he could care less about the facts in BS's book.

OK enough. Going to go clean some more.

What else would you two like to have for eats while you're here. Want to put on my very best effort I'm so excited. I pledge to be on my best behavior because we are so blessed to have you both here at the same time this year.

Love, M

Love, Mom

* * *

mom: Hi child, just thinking, what do you want to do for Mother's Day? I can cook dinner, we can't do brunch due to dad's and his obsession with karate, he has to leave by 10 am

me: dad can skip karate. we're going to brunch and it's not mother's day if you cook. I can bbq at my house though

mom: Sorry, dad won't miss karate except for his funeral, or mine, maybe yours, and he won't leave the house alone either. so BBQ at our house is better, you can bring dessert. I do NOT need any gits, flowers at the most. Save your money, you spend a lot on me already. I need to marry you off in style.

* * *

mom: Hi

me: hey ma

mom: DeeDee had a party at the temple yesterday at 1 pm.
She said it was a purim party and it had nothing to do with purim.

me: no costumes, no hamantaschen?

mom: The food was Italian. It was great tasting. She had as entertainment a Karoke fellow about my age or younger. He came twice before.

Once two years ago when the Rabbi sang bad bad leroy brown and I sang Ooh Ooh Baby Baby. They have to be all tone deaf

because they said I sounded good. I should go on American Idol. Simon would have a field day with me. LOL

me: ohh man

mom: I sang with him before about three years I think it was Tracks of my Tears then. I was thinking what you once told me. Ma don't ever sing in public. I also had a hard act to follow. It was the Rabbi who sang some hebrew songs before me. I told him he is a hard act to follow. Reba fell while dancing. She didn't break anything but is

really sore from the fall. Jacob Steinberg left early because he had a nosebleed.

me: hahahaha

* * *

Well, someone finally said it and there are several videos online (youtube) about Oprah hosting the antichrist (Eckhart Tolle) and the largest church in the world (her online worldwide classroom). I had this feeling about it; I don't know what to think. Did I have that feeling b/c God is speaking to me; and maybe I shouldn't read the book?? Just thought you would find it interesting after our conversation. I'm sure you would have no trouble finding the stuff I've looked at. There's one that is touting a new book called "Don't Drink the Koolaid: Oprah, Obama and Occult" or something like that. I guess I just need to pray and read and keep an open mind (though some say that's dangerous). Just rambling here....

Oh well, so hoping you're doing OK today. I still don't know if you have dental insurance or not b/c I got so caught up in watching videos about The Oprah.

I love you; see you soon, I hope.
mom

* * *

We went to church today. Father said there is a baby alligator in the little pond by the church. He said he wanted everyone to be very careful when they were out there until he gets trained to go to the Presbyterian side of the pond :)

* * *

Subject: Escape from mother's day

hi dear, just got your call after returning home through throngs of be-rouged, over-dressed, corsaged moms smiling through sore feet.

"I Would Like a Goat for Mother's Day"

* * *

I'm on my way out to attend a guest lecture by Bruce Feiler at the Temple Tifereth Israel. I read his two books, Walk the Bible and Abraham. I enjoy his writing style and I hope to get his autograph, acution them off for copious $$$$$ and retire to Colorado. You can come out to ski or snowboard if you like.

Dad is kicking off the fall season by installing a new tile floor in our bathroom. I just cleaned and reorganized the basement so I can sew again. I'm in a throwing out mood.

It's cool and breezy here. I noticed your temp's went waaay down too.

Gotta go. Let's hope al-queda doesn't try and show off tomorrow. We have our flag up!! Stay safe and maybe keep your cute little American face indoors. Love mom

CHAPTER 14

"Remember Me? Your Mother?"

MISSING YOU

BACK IN THE olden days, it was nearly impossible for kids to avoid their mother's probing questions: Pick up the phone (oh, what a great invention you were, caller ID!), and there she was on the line, wondering what happened with the new job, the old boyfriend, the dog, the cat, and why *she* always had to be the one to call. But since it's all too easy these days for kids to avoid their mother's phone calls and delete their voice mails, moms have to resort to electronic communication to make their feelings known. And email is the perfect medium for moms to subtly, or not-so-subtly, remind their kids of their existence. As one mom wrote to her daughter: "Are you swamped? Are you enjoying the sunshine? Do you remember me???"

As communication has changed, moms have been forced to adapt, but it can be a painful process. Many young adults barely talk on the phone anymore, even to their friends or significant others, and most don't even have a landline. So if a mom isn't text-ing or IMing or emailing or leaving comments on her kids' blogs, she might not be able to communicate with her son or daughter at all. And when moms get upset about an unreturned phone call, many kids will protest that they've texted or IMed or emailed or blogged, but to a mom that's no excuse—there'll never be an elec-tronic substitute for actually hearing her child's voice.

* * *

I'm sitting at the computer,
My hair has turned to gray.
Hair is growing from my nose and ears,
But I wait here anyway.
I haven't eaten all day long
I'll probably fade away
But that doesn't really matter.
I'll wait here anyway.
I will not sleep.
I will not poop.
For I choose not to stray.
No matter what befalls me.

I'll wait here anyway.
What causes such devotion?
What makes my cause so just?
I'm waiting for your email.
And I'll wait here til I bust!

Love, Mom

* * *

mom: Good morning.
me: hello!
mom: I'm thinking of maybe flying to Michigan to have dinner with your brother, as dad has band practice for Mother's Day weekend and I don't want to be alone. I wish you, your brother and I could all be to-gether for Mother's Day somehow but you are so far away. So if you are sending anything "alive" for Mother's Day, make sure I'll be here (not to be presumptuous).

* * *

Hi Jane-o:

Are you swamped?

Are you enjoying the sunshine?

Do you remember me???

Love,

Mom

* * *

Subject: I miss you
After our phone call....well, poop on you. I love you anyway!

* * *

I'm on nite shift again, so if you are up at 2 am and want to drunk dial some-one, I'm up! Wed, Thur and Friday nites. Love you, good luck. ? Mom

* * *

Dad and I are worried about you. We haven't heard from you since you called Monday nite to say you ate moldy bread. Please call or let us know every-thing is okay so we can stop worrying.

* * *

ok...you're an NGO founding, leopard hunting, porn star..makes sense..When are you coming home?

* * *

AMANDA, THIS MORNING AROUND 630, I WAS OUTSIDE RAKING SOME LEAVES. ALL OF A SUDDEN, I SAW A NEW PINK GERBER DAISY THAT HAD JUST PEAKED THROUGH THE SURFACE. IT SAID TO ME, "GOODMORNING MOM, IT IS ME, AMANDA" SO THERE.! WHAT A NICE WAY TO START MY DAY!!! AND GOODMORN-ING TO YOU TOO! I LOVE YOU MOM.

* * *

Come Home.

I don't want to have to think of you travelling in remote areas, in big bad cities, on remote islands, on almost deserted beaches, in a unlocked room, on some unsafe plane, train, bus, boat, rickhaw, bike, car, trail, bridge, el-ephant, horse with no one who is practically family watching out for you.

Come Home.

Mom

Love, Mom

* * *

Dearest Sweetnesses, So. Here's the thing: WHY i am getting two copies of all your emails? I'm not understanding this. Why do I have to be told everything two-two times? I must confess, I am intrigued. You, Miss, wish to <u>schedule</u> a pha-mely phone call?? <u>AWWwwww</u>, so cute! Can we schedule this on an ad hoc basis, not ad inifinitum? Phor eczhample, looks like 1 pm this Sunday works for all concerned. Hurray! Oh, Nikhil, why your mocking of your sister? I think you will be very much appreciating pha-mely time phone call. So in conclusion, Nikhil I've sent you granola (it already has bran cereal in it.) and we'll talk on Sunday Be well my little blueberries. I love you! MOM

* * *

What's new lovey? I tried to call you, but you're not around. We are having a great time. Friends and family are lots of fun! It's cold here. What are you going 4th of July? Are you off for a few days? Send me an e-mail and let me know what's going on in your life. I miss you and need to connect. I'll be home Saturday afternoon. Then Yma & Joe are coming Sunday and Monday. I'll be back at work Tuesday. Stay in touch with your mother! I'm needy! love, mom

* * *

It is now Sunday evening and no messages from you since TUESDAY!!! Are you ok? Just write and say busy get back to you or something. Your uncle has returned to Virginia. Now Carole misses him. Go figure.

Your grandmother is positive that some people came in and talked to her and told her she is going to Mexico. They were supposed to come back yesterday evening and take her there. Oops, they didn't show up! Go figure.

I miss being able to just pick up my phone and text you or call you. Go figure.

Love you, Mom

* * *

i just wanted to tell you that I miss you. and i hope when you and Jeff decide to settle down that its here in Chicago. especially when you have a baby. not that im putting any pressure on you.

* * *

I was in hard labor this time 27 years ago begging them to do something. I had been ready to deliver you (completely ready) since 8:30 am and your head was sunnyside up which makes for a tighter delivery. I kept pushing and pushing as

Dr. Ball tried everything to turn you every so slightly. I remember just being very very tired and in hard labor without anything given to me.

I begged for relief and I just kept rolling my head back and forth moaning and begging for that spinal. Well after 2 hours of that, Dr. Ball noticed your heart rate was changing to where they needed to do an emergency c-section. By that time I had gotten a spinal, he quickly opened me up and I heard the most precious little cry out of a girl!!!!! You were a good baby from the very beginning. You had an inexperienced mom which stressed you out at times -- colic. I remember waking your dad up every time I nursed you at night and getting him to help me because I thought you would just break. After 4 weeks of wondering if I was a good mom and had enough milk for you--- your pediatrician looked at me after your checkup and said" I don't know what you are doing- but keep doing it because this little one has gained 3 lbs in 3 weeks. What a difference his words made for me. I felt like I could do this mothering thing!. God gave me such a gift when he gave me you 27 years ago. I love you. MOM

* * *

darling--

 had a signal for 30 seconds today...your mailbox full i think, but i lost the

call anyway. please email me. i miss you desperately and don't do well when
i cannot reach you. i will try one more time, but i have to go stand near a ski
lift with skiers flying by....i even updated my roaming but it does no good!!!!
please write me a long detailed email. i need to hear from you darling.
love and kisses,
mommy

*   *   *

Subject: Remember Me?
Your mother?

Call me.

*   *   *

Sacha schedule:

Today

8am think about mama

9 am go to work?

10 am think about mama

12 mama to call you?

Mama schedule:

8am think about sacha, eat breakfast to include Bear Naked expensive granola, wasabi peas, carrots, celery, bread from yeleshevsky - rye bread

9 am think about sacha

12 call sacha

* * *

I've been trying to call you back all day, but keep getting that message that your voice mail box is not set up - so i can't get in touch. (same thing that happened the other day) so - call me ok? love mom

* * *

me: hi mom, i miss you love you

mom: i miss you too, will you come home after finals????????????????? love mom

me: yes i have hair appts the weekend of may 10th

mom: yeah!!!!!!!!!!!!!! make a dentist appointment

"Remember Me? Your Mother?"

* * *

Dear Julie, Thought I was just letting you know that I enjoy speaking to you and that I miss you. Did not intend to give you guilt. Luv, Mom

* * *

we did "free range parenting."
Also known as "letting children be children." or
"letting children live"
also known as "being sensible"
or "common sense parenting"

xo yer ma

ADVICE FOR MOMS

PROBLEM: Your daughter hasn't emailed you in five days—come to think of it, since she told you she was moving in with a new roommate she met on Craigslist. Should you call her boyfriend? Or maybe the police?

SOLUTION: *There's an axiom that says something to the effect of: "The number of days your child will ignore you is directly proportional to the number of panicky/guilt-tripping emails that you send." (This axiom has held true since the dawn of the Internet.) So if you've been sending your little darlings five or six emails a day with no response, step slowly away from the computer and resolve not to contact them again. Odds are, within the next couple of days, you'll get an email, or maybe even a phone call, from your son or daughter, who's "just calling to check in." (Playing hard to get works with children as well as it does with significant others!) Now, if you really and truly—and be honest!—feel that their lives could be in danger, you hereby have our permission to call the police. But, we warn you, this option can only be used sparingly and in instances of extreme emergency, or else your children will immediately move to a sparsely populated island with no phone service or Internet access, just to torture you.*

CHAPTER 15

"Dad Is Sleeping as He Enjoyed the Whiskey at the Party"

DRINKING, DRUGS,
AND GOOD TIMES

WHO CAN BLAME Mom if she wants to kick back with a goblet of vino after an exhausting day? But sometimes Mom has several glasses of that vino, and other times she takes her drunk ass and starts emailing her children. "per dad I get typer as I get drunk," one tipsy momma babbles. And then, by way of explanation, she writes, "It has been a LONG WEEK AT work!!!!!!!!!! !!!!!!!!!!!!!!!!!!!"

Other moms are teetotalers who use scare tactics to keep their kids off the drugs. "Did you hear about the chick in KC who left her little kid alone, and the kid ate cocaine? Seriously." Some mothers use good ol' passive aggression to keep their children away from the vices of the world. A loving mother suggests her daughter give up smoking for her dad—as a Christmas present.

But many moms are merely curious about the seedy drug

underworld, and now that their kids are safely out of the reach of D.A.R.E. officers, they feel comfortable asking them about it. "How do you take meth?" one inquiring mother wanted to know. "Do you smoke it, eat it, inject it, or inhale it?" (We won't ask why this mom assumed her child would be able to answer this question . . .)

* * *

Hey you guys!! We figured out last night that the real name of this place is "Lost" Cabos. We got sooo wasted last night...keg stands...that it took us an hour to find our car and we had to have the help of Adam and Ricardo even then! Met up with all of the neighbors...had cocktails at Cabo Wabo, ate at Mi Casa, and then went back to Cabo Wabo until we couldn't think. Anyway, lots of whales, no clouds...just beautiful but like Arizona, etc., very dry and brown. You guys write back.

Love to you all...Mom

* * *

At Kaufmann's seder we decided that Adir Hu (after 4 cups of wine) could be a drinking song! The melody had us lifting our glasses and swinging them....

"Dad Is Sleeping as He Enjoyed the Whiskey at the Party"

The other Jewish drinking song (again, appropriate because of the seder and the 4 glasses) : the kiddush!!!!!!!!!!!

LOL!

Mom

* * *

Bromg me your book. Don't want to spend money unless its a keeper.

Oops--make that BRING your book. Ugh--too much wine. By the way, its really good wine.

* * *

DAD IS SLEEPING AS HE ENJOYED THE WHISKEY AT THE PARTY

UNCLE MURRAY AND AUNT BONNIE ARE AT A WEDDING AT THE PIERRE.
I ASKED DAD WHO HE THINKS WILL DRINK MORE,
HE SAID, MURRAY, HANDS DOWN.

* * *

How do you take meth? Do you smoke it, eat it, inject it, or inhale it?

Mom

* * *

I had a dream last night about cussing. The message was that I needed to clean up my language. It was a weird dream but I get the message. So no more shit and damn. Oh, joy. This pisses me off. Oh, no. No more piss either. Oh, joy. So, I am now on the wagon.

Have to go. Type at me later. I enjoy your emails too.

Yo clean mouthed mama

* * *

Call me later if you want to. i MIGHT answer. i LOVE you, and am missing you. we'll get together soon. oh by the way, i'm having that little thing taken off of my nose friday. it's just a small raised place, but because the one on my arm was squamous cell carcinoma they want it off right away. i get to be sedated because i'm a chicken. so i'll be a little drunk friday and maybe saturday. i have a low tolerance remember.

Talk to you later,

Mom

* * *

mom: hi honey. geeeeeeeeeeeeeeeeeeeee!!!! you up late

me: yessssssssssss. ive been to the bars

mom: uh ohhhh. i just emailed Linda. told her about your ball

me: my ball????

mom: huh""""""""""""""""""""""??????

me: wha ?tball

mom: softball

me: ohhhhhhhhhhh

mom: ummmmmmmmmm,,,,,, what are you doing on the puter?

me: i dont know

mom: you shouldn't be typing either, look at your spelling LOL hee hee. dad says gooooo tooo bed

me: i know

are you intoxicated??

mom: wondering myself

me: haha thats good..

mom: my nose is plugged and I can't type

;p;

my fingers are lost

me: where are you why arent you here??

mom: I'm in snow country and my husband won't let me out to play

* * *

Have a wonderful junior year!
1. Don't get murdered
2. Don't get stoned
3. Don't get drunk
4. Have fun:)
I love you,
Mom

* * *

I think I'm gonna cry...

I have the BEST daughter on earth. You have been the ideal child. I am the one who has been blessed.

Now, let's go get drunk.

Love you!
Mommy

* * *

I've been meaning to ask you why you're going to Amsterdam and also where else were you going? And who's going with you?

Did you know (I just found out - Daddy told me) that Amsterdam has legalized prostitution and drugs? I know that you're probably chuckling right now, thinking "Oh, does my mother think I'm going to join a prostitution and drug ring." No, I don't, but I do think that the atmosphere in a country like that is more dangerous. So, you're sitting in a bar and the guy next to you is probably doing drugs. Why are you going there?

I'll talk to you later.

Love ya,

Mom

* * *

came home today and found the funniest thing. on the stairs was a bag and a swirly pipe of some sort. hmmmmmm what could it be???? after much investigating i was led to your closet, to my surprise it looks like the girls were hiding their stash in your closet. can you believe it?????? there was pot all over your floor. they just wanted me to tell you about it and sorry for messing up your room those silly girls

187

Love, Mom

stay warm
and call me or something
love
mom

* * *

I have helped your father drink 4 bottles of wine. (p.s. we have a wine tasting today later...ahahahahahha)   I am trying to figure out my next schedule.. I would like to have your children easter sunday thru wednesday am???????? I have to get Wednesday time approved off.

Anyway,....I hope the idea gets across. per dad I get typer as I get drunk. It has been a LONG WEEK AT work!!!!!!!!!!!!!!!!!!!!!!!!!!!   I think I have Dad convinced to to go semi-nude (retirement) March 2009!!!!!!!!!!!!!!!!!!!!!

Holy crap!!!!!!!!!!!!!!!!!!!!!!!!! AhHHHHHHHHHmENNNNNNNNNNNNNNNNNN

Love you lots ans lots.....

Mrytle

XOXOXOXO

* * *

Bought a 4-pack of Bud Light with Clamato. It also has salt and Lime in it.

Don't get any. It was really kind of funky. The clamato settles to the bottom, but since it's beer, you can't shake it up to mix it.

Weeerd. He thought it would be like Corona with a lime.

Duh, read the label, C-l-a-m-a-t-o.

Oh, well, won't have another one of those.

Have only had 2 beers here. But I'm ok with that. These aren't beery people.

Having Fun! It's all in the attitude. Love, yomama

* * *

What are you doing for Easter? Be careful when you stay with these "internet" friends. I'm sure that most of them are respectable people...but there are assholes everywhere. Even in the Indie Pop scene. Be careful that no one has the opportunity to put anything in your drink. What if they pressure you for sex? These are older men who have years of experience. Not everyone has good intentions. Just be careful. You've been lucky so far, but there are people who will try to take advantage of you in some way. Just be aware of this. Don't get mad at me for saying for these things. It's my motherly duty. You'll understand someday when you have children of your own.

Love, Mom

* * *

Thanks for the photo!

D's guy looks surly and unhappy – too bad, life is short.

Your guy looks pleasant and charming, and reminds me of Tim Robbins (or whatever Susan Sarandon's companion is named). You already know where I stand on the smoking, drinking, and tats.

My favorite part was seeing your lovely face (quelle surprise). I notice that your hair is longish again – are you in between cuts, growing out, or just over short hair? Whichever, I like the look.

I'm interested in hearing about the drama that led to the loss of your phone. Send the bill to D's husband.

I'm mailing you a package today.

Are you off on Monday, and do you have big weekend plans?

Thanks again, and have a great day.

I love you– Mom

CHAPTER 16

"OK I Had the Wendy Is Pregnant Dream"

ANALYZING THE SUBCONSCIOUS

ORGET FREUD, JUNG, and all those other revered head-shrinkers. Moms know that when they really want insight into what's going on in their subconscious, they've got to turn to their kids. (After all, they're the ones with the expensive liberal arts educations.) Moms' dreams run the gamut: from dreams about teeth (very Freudian) to dreams about pregnancy (very, uh, obvious). Sometimes dreams can bring up truths we'd rather not acknowledge, and so a mom telling her daughter she had a dream that her son lost his job and no one told her just *might* be a sign that she's feeling distance from her children. Or take this mom, who wrote: "I had a dream the other night that I got married again and right at the end of the ceremony someone came in and blew up everything. Everyone was killed beside me the groom and then he and I both suspected each other of being behind the whole thing. What do you think are the Freudian implications of that? Good?"

We're going to have to go with: probably not.

* * *

dear ones,

be careful. who knows whether these dreams of Mom mean anything? but last night, i did dream about her--nothing memorable, just her presence. i don't think the dream refers to me although i still have bronchitis. (thank you to lois for her house call and for her cough medicine; i'm getting looser and coughing less.) i hope everything is good for you. be careful of speeding cars (yours and others), dark streets, tsunames, neighbors' weimarners, flirtatious co-workers, and anything else.

love,

mama

ps. let me know that you're ok.

* * *

Having very strange dreams. In one my teeth were grinding up, and I was spitting out little pieces. (They are pulling those 2 the 12th). In another I had a 3rd eye. I was freaking out because I thought it had just popped up; then

"OK I Had the Wendy Is Pregnant Dream"

I realized it had been under my bangs where it didn't show. It was small and had little bitty lashes and seemed to be asleep. Love you,

Mom

* * *

I had a dream about you last night, I went over to see you and you told me that you decided to grow a monobrow, like Salma Hayek in "Frida" http://monobrow.com/ It was growing very nicely. I thought, oh good, what the hell could possibly be next????????????....LOLOLOL

* * *

Ok I had the Wendy is pregnant dream. I will keep you imformed. THe dream also had a snake that crawled up on Rebecca's head and liked her hair. SHe didn't die of fright so I think she likes snakes.
Mom

* * *

help me with this one....
last night i dreamed that mark got fired but no one told me for a while......

i also had a dream that i knew that paul zimmerman was planning to bomb a major building-it was like the congress building-and i was there. he had flowers delivered that a bomb was inside. i knew about it and didn't alert anyone and many people died.

any insight into either of these?

* * *

mom: gtg... congrats... you are MY amazing kid... i am very happy and proud, lots of bragging rights

me: bye

mom: oh... i dreamed about oliver last nite... he kept biting my hand while i was trying to sleep... that was the dream

weird, huh?

me: yep

mom: bye...

* * *

I had a dream the other night that I got married again and right at the end of the ceremony someone came in and blew up everything. Everyone was killed beside me the groom and then he and I both suspected each other of being behind the whole thing. What do you think are the Freudian implications of that? Good?

Also, I found your passport.

-mom

* * *

if you have a minute, call me at home. i was hoping you could help me with dream analysis....

* * *

me: Obv. Jenna had a dream last night that she was a black lady running through the fields with a white baby she thought was hers.

mom: It's a symbol of her love confusion—subconsciously weighing seemingly conflicting feelings when if she would just admit to the blatantly clear, all would merge into a cohesive image...

me: That is way out, mama.

mom: Not really. One has to own one's feelings, after all, or they will manifest in unusual and troubling ways.

* * *

Hi Honey! It was SO good talking to you last night. I do miss chatting with you and having a good political discussion. I had the funniest dream the other night that I was at some social gathering and George Stephanopoulos was there with his wife. I was mentioning how much we liked his book and you were rolling your eyes at me. J Barbara Walters was there too and we were on a first name basis—she was very nice. Oh well—I woke up.

Mom

* * *

We saw Third by Wendy Wasserstein last night. really really enjoyed her last play. as we left, dad said that you could write something like that.

then i had a dream about mara stein. she married someone else. someone she had met at a NASCAR race. talk about random.

how's everyone?

* * *

OK on top of worrying about you considerably the last two days I dream last night that my doctor was putting the moves on me and when I went to see him he turned into Javier Bardem

 **MOVIE MOMS**

Infinitely quotable and always memorable, the silver-screen moms on this list have made a major imprint on modern cinema. Some of them are based on real-life mommas, while others have a supernatural bent, and only one of them resorted to capital punishment. Despite their disparate mothering styles, they all have one thing in common: their revered place in the pop-culture pantheon.

Mrs. Robinson, *The Graduate*

Long before the term "cougar" entered the lexicon, Mrs. Robinson (Anne Bancroft) was working her sexual magic on hapless recent college grad Ben Braddock and making stockings look just about as hot as they've ever looked. While she is probably not the ideal momma—what with all the lying and the manipulation and having sex with her daughter's beau—her sexual adventurousness and housewifely discontent get Mrs. Robinson points for being emblematic of the turbulent late '60s.

Elaine Miller, **Almost Famous**

A delightful blend of intellectualism, second-wave feminism, and a dash of overprotection, professor Elaine Miller (Frances McDormand) grudgingly allowed her prodigiously talented fifteen-year-old, William, to follow a band touring around the country for *Rolling Stone.* Elaine regrets her permissiveness almost instantly, and at one point yells to a classroom full of students, "Rock stars have kidnapped my son!"

Joan Crawford, **Mommie Dearest**

If the movie version of the memoir by Christina Crawford about her mother, Joan (Faye Dunaway), is anywhere near the truth, then Joan held more than a modicum of evil in those signature arched eyebrows. Lil' adopted Christina was in for a doozy of an upbringing by unhinged, fame-hungry Joan—a childhood that included a lot of physical abuse and a boatload of cruel manipulation. But at least one good thing came out of all that upset: the phrase "no more wire hangers" and its place in the pop-cultural lexicon.

Rachel Flax, **Mermaids**

Cher was oh-so-glamorous as single mom Rachel in *Mermaids,* and even though her nomadic lifestyle raised the ire of her older daughter, Charlotte (a very cute and very young Winona Ryder), she always knew how to have *fun.* Rachel serves meals made exclusively of cocktail appetizers and loves to get dressed up, be it in her daily outfits or in—what else?—a mermaid costume for Halloween. Though her mothering techniques were unorthodox, particularly for the time (the movie is set against the 1963 Kennedy assassination), Rachel's ebullience keeps this film floating in warm and fuzzy territory.

Mrs. Banks, **Mary Poppins**

This beautiful suffragist played with pep by Glynis Johns is so busy getting women the right to vote that she enlists the help of supernatural nanny Mary Poppins (the angelic Julie Andrews) to help wrangle her wee ones. As we all know, Mary Poppins made Mrs. Banks realize that she had to spend more time bonding with her children, Jane and Michael, which goes to show that even turn-of-the-century mums struggled with finding a work/life balance.

Margaret White, **Carrie**

Probably the most awful of the mothers listed (even worse than ol' "wire hangers"), Margaret White (Piper Laurie) used her fanatical religiosity to keep Carrie (Sissy Spacek) on a short leash—and punish her for her telekinesis. After Carrie goes bonkers on prom night, Margaret tries stabbing her only daughter. But you don't mess with the kids with supernatural powers: Solely through the power of her mind, Carrie rounds up all the knives in the house and crucifies her mother against the living room door. Yikes!

Aurora Greenway, **Terms of Endearment**

Men love Aurora (Shirley MacLaine), but her daughter, Emma (Debra Winger), loves and hates her in equal measures. And for good reason: Aurora is a meddling, controlling, all-around pain in the ass. But this Southern belle is also a fiercely loyal mom, who would probably kill a man with her bare hands for messing with her only Emma.

Manuela, **All About My Mother (Todo Sobre Mi Madre)**

After her son Esteban dies tragically in Madrid, Manuela (Cecilia Roth) goes back to her roots in Barcelona, in part to find her son's father...who is now a transvestite. Through a series of coincidences and tragedies, Cecilia ends up raising another Esteban, and showing that the power of mother-love knows bounds greater than blood.

Stifler's Mom, American Pie

Mrs. Stifler likes her scotch like she likes her men: aged eighteen years. Played by the pillow-lipped, curvaceous comedian Jennifer Coolidge, Mrs. Stifler helped usher in an updated term for what used to be called a Mrs. Robinson: MILF.

M'Lynn Eatenton, Steel Magnolias

The prim matriarch of a sprawling Southern family, M'Lynn Eatenton (Sally Field) rules her roost with charm and a well-shellacked helmet of hair. She's long-suffering and well mannered—and she's always there to be the voice of reason for her more free-spirited kin. When tragedy strikes M'Lynn (and in this kind of tearjerker, tragedy is a necessary plot point), she handles it with grace and the help of the biddies over at her local beauty shop (played by Dolly Parton, Shirley MacLaine, Olympia

Dukakis, and Daryl Hannah). When Dolly Parton is your best buddy, how can you not feel better?

Honorary Mention: Auntie Mame, Auntie Mame

Even though Auntie Mame isn't an actual mom, she deserves a mention on this list because she takes over mothering duties and because Rosalind Russell portrayed her with such fabulous hilarity. Who else would let her adopted son attend a bohemian nudist elementary school?

CHAPTER 17

"I've Been Assuming That You Are without Internet, Not That Your Plane Was Hijacked by Mutant Dingos"

TRAVEL AND FAMILY VACATIONS

MOTHERS ARE OVERLY concerned about the well-being of their children even when they live in the same house. When their kids are thousands of miles away, the worrying reaches a fever pitch. They imagine scenarios in which their wayward daughters end up in Kafkaesque lockdown in faraway countries. "Don't accept ANYTHING from ANYONE to bring back," one mom admonishes. "It might be stuffed with drugs and you will get caught and have to spend 25 years in a Thai jail !!!!!"

And when not obsessing about the worst-case situations for their children in foreign lands, moms are terrified of the planes taking themselves abroad. Some tell their kids where to find copies of their living wills and where they've stashed the valuables. One mom sends this memo from the airport: "Mechanical problems........keep me in your prayers."

Once vacationing moms get off the plane and arrive at their

final destinations, they really start living it up. They sneak out in the middle of the night, they eat crème brûlée with reckless abandon, and ride around in convertibles with movie-star sunglasses. But vacation time for empty-nesters doesn't just mean weeks off gallivanting by themselves. Many moms love to plan family vacays, and once Mom has decided to play cruise director for the entire clan, there is no end to her planning. One mom sends a detailed fourteen-item "Vacation Packing List" so that her daughters don't forget anything important like a toothbrush or underwear. But even with a tinge of mom OCD, it's still a vacation. "They have an AMAZING frozen yogurt machine here," one momma boasts; everyone knows it's not a real vacay without superlative fro-yo.

* * *

I am delayed at airport.

Now if the plane goes down, turn my body to diamonds and buy me a new outfit. One that makes my butt look small.

Love all of you.......good bye.

PS. Mechanical problems........keep me in your prayers.

* * *

Danielle - be sure to drink a lot of water on your flight .... keeps nose and throat moist, and wards off infection. Planes have very dry air, and dry air invites cooties into the nasal passage. and I know you won't don a face mask, so hydrate ,hydrate.

try to let me know when you arrive
love mom

* * *

Hi Sweetie,

So glad I can email without worry! What's a "Gaudí"? Sounds intriguing. An international adapter sounds like a good call. This will not be your last adventure so there's a great chance you will use it for many more occasions.

No surprise on the Sunday closure. When your Dad & I did our whirlwind continental excursion we arrived in Florence mid morning Saturday & left Monday morning. Not much to do when the whole city closed for Siesta Saturday afternoon, re-opened in the evening but was closed the whole next day. So sad! I think the Spanish & Italian are similar in that respect.

xoxox

mom

* * *

how are you? what's going on in nyc? The cruise ship is nice but small and not as much food as the last one. We we are having a wonderful time -- too bad for youuuuuuuuuuuuuuuuuuuuuuu.... hahaha.

I got sick the first night and puked. Feel better now, thank God. They have an AMAZING frozen yogurt machine here -- fat free and the most delicious ever -- very tcbyish - unfortunately, they just shut the damn thing off and I didn't get to have one today -- bastards. So I hope work is getting better and easier. Love you and miss you. See you Saturday.

MOM

* * *

I'm already planning all your favourite meals -- roast dinner with all the trimmings, apple crumble, cake, yellow chicken (or Quorn if your still veggie??!!). Don't forget what I told you about looking after your luggage! Don't accept ANYTHING from ANYONE to bring back to UK ....it might be stuffed with drugs and you will get caught and have to spend 25 years in a Thai jail !!!!!

Can't wait to see you.

Love you loads xxxxxxxxxxxxxxxxxxxxxxxxxxxxxxxxxxxxxxxxxxxxxxxxxxxxxxxxxxxxxxx xxxxxxxxxxxxxxxxxxxxxxxxxxxxxxxxxxxxxxxxxxxxxxxxxxxxxxxxxxxxxxxxxxxxxxxxxxx xx

* * *

Phuket is gorgeous and it's a cheap trip, why don't you guys pack up and meet us? We've still got 15 days before we leave. Oh yeah, Timmy doesn't have a passport yet and maybe Thailand isn't a great place for a baby. Well, next time then. Bob and Yvette are no fun so last night Paul and I said we were going back to the room to rest after dinner and snuck out to go have fun, almost got busted by a baby elephant eating bananas blocking the street exit though....close call!

Love you,
mom

Love, Mom

* * *

The moblie ICU and I made it here! I am wearing shorts and sweating in the shade. It is too cold, though, for ocean swimming or even pool swimming. However, I am really enjoying the culture. We are staying in a more or less authenic place (ie you have to boil the water!) where the courtyard is draped with bougainville flowers. We have found the localeateries and festivals as opposed to the more specifically American places. You can see the economy is on the upswing--locals wearing orthodontia, for example. WalMart, Costco, and Home Depot are here, too. We bought our water at WalMart. I have not figured out how to retrieve voice mail. I have figured out how to call back.

I love you all!

* * *

Being we are traveling by plane I should tell you my jewelry is in the bank and the keys are in Dad's dresser. He started on his income tax and everything is in the den.

I usually tell Tina all this as she was closer to home but being she is traveling by plane too I thought I would impart some of this information to you. Tina says I get paranoid when I travel by plane.

Looking forward to seeing all of you.

Love, MOM

* * *

Hello, Sweetie! I hope you are having a big time in Australia!! It's
Thanksgiving here, and we are thankful you are having a great adventure!
I've been assuming that you are without internet, not that your plane was
hijacked by mutant dingos.

Well, take care of yourself and have a great time.
We love you lots!!!!
Hugs from afar--
Mom

* * *

I'll ask Dad his thoughts and let you know (he's asleep in a blue chair right
now). My only problem with Hawaii is the long plane ride, but with drugs I
might be okay. It can't hurt to explore either option, and they both sound
good to me (with me magically appearing in Hawaii). Thanks for thinking of
choices. And thanks for the call last night.

I love you- Mom

CHAPTER 18

"Charlie Has
Exploding
Anal Glands"

PETS, ANIMALS,
AND THEIR ALL-TOO-FREQUENT
BOWEL MOVEMENTS

I T'S PRETTY CLEAR that pets often serve as surrogate children, especially after the kids (finally) leave the nest. But some moms take this act of transference just a little too far and, of course, mix it in with a healthy dose of guilt. After getting a new dog, one mom tells her daughter over instant messenger, "I gave her your name because you aren't around much any more." Besides, once the kids are out of the house, that means moms have more money to spend on their four-legged friends, as one mom writes: "I am calling a personal dog trainer. Pam had revealed she sent her Jack Russell a few yrs ago to doggie boot camp for 2 wks ($ 1200)." Even moms who don't use their pets as direct child substitutes or guilt conveyors tend to be obsessed with the minutiae of their animals' everyday lives. And by minutiae, we mean poop. Roombas do *not* successfully clean cat diarrhea, one mom writes in an email. Then there's the mom with a depressed cat; she tells her kids that she's on her fourth bottle of carpet cleaner (no additional details needed).

It all leads one to wonder: If email had existed when these moms first had babies, would they be emailing *their* mothers with the up-to-the-minute details of their children's bowel movements? (Actually, they'd probably take a cue from the thousands of parents who have been compelled to chronicle every burp and fart by their newborn and start a baby blog.)

* * *

frankie got out of the fence today. that dumb dog made me so mad@#!!! i was feeding the horses some apples and then he got out of the fence so I threw all the apples at the horses and ran after him, fell, cut my nose, then decided he wasn't worth it and walked back to the house. got in the car and he wasn't too far, bribed him with a treat and then locked him in the wood-shop 'cause i was so mad. i was finally speaking to him when i came to work.

* * *

FYI: I used you as a reference for a puppy application.

If someone calls your cell phone asking for Christine Newsom don't be surprised.

I will forward the info I sent her so you can be on board with my answers.

Don't be alarmed...some info is altered to fit what she "thinks" makes a good home.

Let me know if you have any questions.

* * *

I chased a cow the other day when I was walking.

I was walking by the farm up on top of the hill and I looked up to see a LARGE calf trotting toward me. There was a hill between us that I did not think she would try to come down, but I was startled and I started to turn around. Then I thought, I have to tell them that their cow is out. I shouted "Hey, your cow is loose" and started to walk toward their house. Then I saw the owner and he told me he is trying to wean the calf from its mother, and she is all confused.

So was I!

* * *

Dad uncovered a gerbil skull in the garden. Does anyone want it? It has no teeth. It has been cleaned.

* * *

We got aroma therapy for the cats today- It's suppose to calm them when new animals or people enter their world- Preparation for when you and the dog arrive this week..Jill brought home a golden lab puppy to "visit"--the most mellow puppy that I have ever seen and the baby cat freaked....the other cat (the black one) was distressed that I would not let her snuggle at my head last night--too close for my allergies- so she proceeded to puke all over the hall and my bedroom--ANIMALS>>>>>>>>>>>>>>>>Can't wait to see you..Travel safe..
Love Mom

* * *

Something My Roomba Does Not Clean Well...

Cat diarrhea.

We noticed this AM that Nimby, the cat, had a bit of a digestive upset, as evidenced by the foul stench from under his tail. Shelly held him while I cleaned him up and gave him some medicine. I cleaned the cat box, but still a stinky smell persisted.

In the meantime, Shelly started up the Roomba to vacuum the bedrooms. It finished her bedroom and shot over into mine. Shelly left to go to the mall with her friend. The smell got worse so I concluded that Nimby must have had some diarrhea somewhere other then the litter box. (The last time he did this, it was in the middle of my dry-clean only comforter.) So I headed for the bedroom, where I found Roomba valiantly trying to clean up some of the stinkiest cat diarrhea ever, mainly by spreading it all over the floor and under the dresser. So I grabbed poor Roomba, turned it off, and contemplated my plan of action.

First I took Roomba to the front porch, so I could deal with it later. Then I wiped up what I could in the bedroom with a about half a roll of paper towels.

Then I decided it would be best if I had a snack and watched some TV while I decided what to do. This took about an hour. Initially, I wanted to sell the house and move somewhere else immediately. Then I decided I could clean everything up but would need to buy a new Roomba. Then I decided to I could clean Roomba too.

Fortified, I then took some orange scented floor cleaner, the mop and some more paper towels and cleaned until no more brown smears appeared on the paper towels. The smell was much improved.

Then there was the problem of the Roomba itself. I disassembled all that I could and cleaned it off thoroughly in the laundry sink in the dog room. It was pretty bad. I found out that Roomba had picked up some larger chunks as well.

Finally, I soaked my hands in Clorox Clean Up and water for about 3 minutes, which is when I felt the skin start to peel off.

* * *

I guess whatever you want to buy her is your decision...so...she is sooooo tiny that the XS will probably fit her. She's is a little "tasmanian devil" you know. I'll go downstairs and try to pick her up and she just runs circles around me. Finally, at some point, I'll snatch her up and kiss all over her. But..........no more rawhide bones for her. She threw up yesterday and I think she's too little for that kind of stuff. One more advice: when you go to sleep, you should put all of her toys away. This way she'll learn that sleep time is SLEEP TIME -- for both you and her. She might not be happy for a few days, but eventually when she notices her toys are gone--it's time to relax. You have to teach her that. She is way toooooooo hyper. And you could change that. She needs to listen to you. Anyway, good luck, and I'll see you Friday.

Love, MOM

* * *

Subject: your stupid dog

I thought you'd like to know that Sandy ate a huge piece of crap this morning before I could pull him away. It was probably half-frozen, so he was able to pick it up. Even though I yelled at him, he wouldn't put it down. I would have thrown up if I'd had anything in my stomach. I was so furious with him, and now I have to watch out for all the crap along the way on our walks. I made him stay outside for most of the day. Guess I'll have to feed him earlier now so I can walk him before dark. Sorry to go on and on about this, but I needed to vent. I need to find out if there's anything to give dogs to suppress their appetites, but I doubt there is – and he's only getting worse!

* * *

Hello:

We are going to have another hot day here today, near ninety. That squirrel *just has to take a trip somewhere. We had a squirrel that was a pest when we lived on Colorado Street. He would hang on the screen door. One day I saw that he had an infection in his eye, and I of course, treated it with eye drops. I just waited until he got in the correct position, and squirted the drops right threw the screen into his eye. Now, I cannot tell you if this helped because we moved shortly after this medical event. We got a call yesterday from St Vincent De Paul and thought they wanted a donation when in fact, they wanted an electrician. Dad is going to instill some exit lights and some outside lighting. I bet he will have some stories after he works there. It is located on Franklin Ave. on the east side of town near the old Anglos restaurant. Let us know all of the news about Chats the squirrel. Have a good day.*

Love,

MOM

* * *

me: guess what! stephanie and i are gonna get a pet fish, maybe even two

mom: that should be cute

me: i know

mom: you can keep them in the toilet

save on fish food

me: what, they would eat our poop or something?

mom: its the circle of life....

me: unique idea

i already know what i'm going to name mine

mom: poop eater?

Poopee mange?

i have to get some food

* * *

Munchkins,

I thought Em looked great! Keep her that way. I'm sure she's much healthier now. Well, really, locked in a cage in terror and your own excrement is probably not the way to lose weight, However, now that it's done it would be super if she could stay that way. I think she looks nice---AND I will vow not to fatten her up if she ever stays with me again. It's not going to be hard for her to gain weight again quickly...she already has those fat cells. Enough advice from the overfeeding mamma.

Susan and I have tried to call, but I think either you guys work late or are so social that you are never home. We're going on Wednesday to the Holocaust Museum ---with Adriane as well. Should be a fun little outing. We have yukky old snow here and possibly more on the way. Oh yes, I sent your contacts priority and you should have them asap! They promised 5 day delivery. Well, that's all the news from Lake Wobegon-----where all the dogs are below average and wet their beds every night...

Jamama

* * *

My friend the backyard squirrel has suddenly gone from looking robust to becoming downright tubby. He/she trucks around the yard and rests after each leap forward. A younger squirrel who looks bedraggled and who is chased away by the trucklike squirrel can jump really high with each leap as he crosses the grass. I'm afraid that the tubby squirrel will fall off of the fence. He/she is really fat now - just within the last few days. I've gotten some inexpensive peanuts at Cosco and that may be adding to the problem. Maybe it's diet time for the squirrel.

or, maybe some little squirrels are on the way!

* * *

Well, I took Austin to the vet today because things just keep getting worse. He is now officially clinically depressed. He is on an antidepressant. The vet says that physically he is fine. It is all in his little pea brain (my words). So, he also has to be put in his crate with a bed and a litterbox--no extra room where he can pee/poop. Of course, the crate I have is too small for the litterbox so I have to go buy another one tomorrow. He can come out to play when I am right there watching him every second. He can come out to eat. I'll keep water in the crate. The vet says it could take many weeks to get him straightened out. I'm on my 4th bottle of carpet cleaner. I live to clean up after Austin. Anyway, he goes back in a month. When I put Austin in his carrier to go to the vet, Butterscotch climbed on top of the carrier, and thus on top of Austin, and started jumping up and down.....Love, Mom

* * *

mom: I got a new dog!

me: What did you name it?

mom: I gave her your name because you aren't around much any more.

me: You named your dog after me?

mom: Yes, are you mad?

me: No, it's just odd.

mom: It's not odd. I love that name.

me: You named your dog after your kid

mom: I can never do anything right

* * *

Subject: IRREGULARITIES MY DOO-DOO BUTT!

Daddy and I were a little concerned that mei ling did not doo-doo for two days and she did it on the third day (yesterday). This am she did do it on the deck early..but no wee wee yet.

Then dad came down the stairs this am and looks to the left of the stairs while walking down and yells "Marg..come here" and there was a doo-doo by the fireplace in the living room (regular) ; in another section of the covered rug..a wee-wee; and in another section of the covered plastic, a diarrhea. It took me a half an hr to clean it all up and soften it and I was late for work by 10 min. I told Sam she either slipped by, when I left a little barrier open or she cleverly jumped over a little soda box and now thinks that is here area. She will now have to stay in her crate if we can't watch her.

I am calling a personal dog trainer. Pam had revealed she sent her Jack Russell a few yrs ago to doggie boot camp for 2 wks ($ 1200) .

Mom

* * *

Charlie has exploding anal glands..... all cleaned out at the vet, on antibiotics and is now wearing Penny's E collar.

Yuk!
love Mom

* * *

The cat mystery continues. The other day I trailed her for about three blocks before losing her. One guy, upon whose door I knocked, suggested I put a note on her collar so whoever (or is it whomever) else owns her could give me a call. That would be a good trick if I could touch her but even after almost a year of feeding her I haven't been able to lay a finger on her. She doesn't wear a collar either. Cat of mystery – that's what we call her.

I better go now – I must have something to do,

Love, MOM

CHAPTER 19

"I Hope You Have a Hat with Ears"

WEATHER,
STAYING WARM,
AND REMEMBERING
YOUR GALOSHES

THERE'S ONE ASPECT of their children's lives that mothers will never be able to control, and that's the weather. Moms are regular Al Rokers, giving their children weather updates and telling them to dress properly for the coming rain, snow, or sunshine. Though children might roll their eyes when moms tell them to bring a sweater, deep down they know they'll be happy to have a fuzzy cover-up when the temperature plummets, just as Mom warned it would.

Not only do moms love storm-tracking for their children, but they also seem to adore a weather-based double entendre. One mom gives new meaning to the word "windy" and another feels the need to mention that she's getting three to six inches . . . of snow. But really, why would anyone want to simply look out the window when they could be getting a meteorology report from a patented Doppler Mom-dar.

Love, Mom

* * *

Oh boy – you sound happy – sorry the weather stinks maybe the weekend will be better. I hope the only exercise you're getting isn't walking bar to bar. I'll call you tomorrow – Mom

* * *

Hi Cait ~ Have you seen the weather report for this weekend??? Snow, sleet, COLD! I do want to visit, but not too much walking around. Or how about the following weekend, for my birthday! That could be fun. I haven't spoken to the folks yet, but I will, then I'll call you. Get back to me if you can. Have fun tonight. Mom I was interrupted...did I send this already?

* * *

I'm still in the bathroom!!!! I DID call you back! How are you? How is the weather? Not bad here yet. We have a couple inches of slush and maybe we'll get 5 inches today, It'll have to get colder for that to happen. Your car is being fixed. Needs an alternator and also a timing belt. Just a quick $1000!!!

More babbling later. I'm out of toilet paper!!!

MOMMO

* * *

Yes, I am a pest, but I just looked at Iowa weather and it will be 5 below Tuesday night. Hope you have a hat with ears. Love you, Mom

* * *

So how is the weather in Fargo actually? This morning Hannah said it was fine, and roads were good, and about an hour ago our UPS man said Jamestown had 4 or 5 inches of snow and more coming down. Dad thinks he will be able to come, so if the roads are okay we'll be leaving about 5:30. I'm gonna be SO PISSED if we have to cancel, winter and anything that even hints of it sucks!

Thanks for the emails, I sure get a kick out of your creative finds! Love you honey, and really hope I'll see you tonight, your mom.

* * *

It might be raining after work so wear your galoshes. I'm glad you worked things out, talk, talk, talk, and don't go to bed mad, catch more flies with honey, all in the tone it's said. Love you bunches.

* * *

Love, Mom

I'll tell you our news such as it is. The Conservatory is nearly finished. It has rained a lot and it is raining today. It was fun when we had snow last month. (not fot those who had to go to work.) The dog's tail seems to be getting better. He still sicks-yeeuuk yeeuuk yeeuuk!!!

I went to the hospital and have been signed off for my finger but am still receiving physio. Dad is still busy with E-bay, writing letters of complaint and making cups of tea for the workmen.

I am drinking a cup of peppermint tea as I am quite windy at the moment.

With lots and lots of love and looking forward to seeing you in April.
Mum. XXXXXXXXXXX

* * *

I forgot to tell you. When you come to visit me this summer you will find many flowers. Some how this year my flowerpots are doing much better. I rescued one tropical plant from Wal-Mart (75% off) and It so beautiful!!!!

I will get you a nice pot and plants you can keep in your balcony during the warm months and indoor during winter,

I am out of my mind with so much free time. It rained a lot last night and still is raining more.

Oh well,

Love, your mom

* * *

Yes, it's snowing and we/I might get about 3 to 6 inches...of snow that is....

* * *

Piggy, how was your blizzard ???? They keep mentioning Denver, and showing mega amounts of snow, but I don't know where you are in relation to Denver . Hope you're still happy there and getting lots of snowboarding / sleep / chocolate. I tried to break into your facebook but it wouldn't accept the address/password.Your E mail address WAS wrong in my address book so hopefully this will get to you this time . I'm going to Macleay tomorrow for 2 days, so I hope I hear from you when I get back........have a lovely white Xmas little Pig and know I'm thinking of you with love xxxxxxxxxxxxxxxxMumblesxxxxxx

* * *

Good morning my darlings,

Just wanted to share with you - this morning looking out our kitchen window the sun was coming up and on the snow there was such a glitter of color -

mostly greenish/blue and a rose red sparkling throughout the backyard - it was incredible to see. It was like a stream of Christmas lights were placed on the snow. So beautiful.

amore e pace,

m

* * *

are you having massive weather system? Dad says you are- can't im you- Dad says wear a rain jacket!!!
XXXX

* * *

We are up and watching the weather as it is coming in. Probably will at least lose power. Just wanted you to know in case it turns out to be pretty destructive that are watching and are not being caught off guard.

Will ck with you both later today.

Mom

ps, love you

The History of Moms

Eve: The original mother, she bore some very thankless children. After her son Cain killed her other son Abel and Cain was cast out to wander the desert, do you think he ever wrote? Never!

3000 BC

Lei Zu: According to legend, this Chinese empress discovered silkworms and invented the production of raw silk. Her daughters never liked any of the dresses she made them.

1479 BC

Hatshepsut: The fifth Pharaoh of ancient Egypt, Hatshepsut enjoyed a prosperous rule. She had one daughter, Neferure, and always described herself as the most beautiful of women, which was a lot to live up to for poor Neferure.

842 BC

Athaliah: After the death of her son in this year, Athaliah killed everyone else in the royal family (including, legend says, her grandchildren) to usurp the throne of Judah. After seven years she was deposed and Athaliah's murderous reign ended. What do you expect from a daughter of Jezebel?

ca. 500 BC

Jocasta: The mythological mother of Oedipus, Jocasta was cursed and therefore destined to sleep with and marry her biological son. When Jocasta discovered that she loved her son a little too much, she killed herself, and Oedipus poked his own eyes out.

69 BC

Cleopatra: Another lady Pharoah, born in '69 (BC, that is), Cleo had three children with Roman leader Marc Antony—Alexander Helios, Ptolemy Philadelphus, and Cleopatra Selene II—and one with Julius Caesar, Caesarion. Cleo had originally been married to her brother Ptolemy, but left him for the succession of Roman hotties. Antony also left a wife for Cleo, and when Cleo killed herself by letting an asp bite her, Caesarion was executed for attempting to take power, and Marc Antony's long-suffering wife, Octavia Minor, had to take care of her other kids.

39 BC

Livia Drusilla: Livia Drusilla became the wife of Roman Emperor Augustus in this year. She had two sons from a previous marriage, Tiberius and Drusus. She lobbied extremely hard for her sons' ascent to power, and rumor was that Livia killed Augustus's favorite nephew, Marcellus, as well as Octavian's adopted sons, Lucius and Gaius, so her babies could seize the throne. When Tiberius came to power, do you think he was grateful to his mother? No. He moved to Capri so he wouldn't have to deal with Livia anymore. He didn't even attend her funeral and sent Caligula to give the eulogy. Jerk.

AD 1145

Eleanor of Aquitaine: Queen of both France and England at different points, Eleanor led a Crusade and spent much of her later life in prison for helping one of her sons in his attempt to overthrow his father, the King of England. She had ten children in all—two by the King of France, Louis VII, and eight by the King of England, Henry II. Her son Richard the Lionheart would go on to be king of England; he was his mother's favorite and also probably gay. Coincidence?

1492

Queen Isabella I of Spain: She financed Christopher Columbus's journey to the New World in this year. But in the same year she also instituted that pesky Spanish Inquisition and drove out or killed a lot of Jews and Muslims. She had five children—four girls, including Catherine of Aragon, who would become Henry VIII's first wife, and Joanna "the Mad."

1759

Mary Wollstonecraft: Best known for her treatise *A Vindication of the Rights of Woman* (1796) and as the mother of Mary Shelley, the author of *Frankenstein*. Wollstonecraft had a shotgun wedding to Mary's father, proto-anarchist William Godwin. She argued that education makes women better wives and mothers, and died giving birth to little Mary.

1837

Queen Victoria: Victoria reigned as Queen of England for more than sixty years, beginning in 1837. She bore nine children between the years 1840 and 1857, none of whom ever remembered her birthday. Despite seven attempts on her life throughout her reign and her subjugation of many sad imperial colonies, Victoria was a much-loved leader in her day.

1850

Harriet Tubman: Harriet Tubman helped thousands of slaves escape to the North through the underground railroad. She served as a nurse during the Civil War and was an early cougar, marrying a vet named Nelson Davis twenty years her junior in the post-bellum days and adopting a baby girl named Gertie.

1903

Marie Curie: Marie Curie won the first of her two Nobel Prizes in this year, for physics. In 1910, she won the Nobel Prize for Chemistry. She had two daughters, Eve and Irène, with husband and fellow scientist, Pierre. Her daughters were always nagging her to come outside of that dingy laboratory to play.

1945

Eleanor Roosevelt: First lady par excellence, Eleanor became a UN delegate in 1945 and served until 1952. She had six children, five of whom survived into adulthood. In the midst of their tumultuous adulthoods, the Roosevelt kids managed to have nineteen marriages, fifteen divorces, and twenty-nine children.

1979

Margaret Thatcher: Margaret Thatcher was elected prime minister of England. The old iron lady served the Tories for over a decade. She has two children, Mark and Carol, and there's a nectarine named after her in South Africa.

1996

Madonna: Shocking the world by becoming a momma herself, Madonna gave birth to Lourdes on October 14 of this year. She shocked the world even further by seeming to be a pretty decent and normal mom to Lourdes, and later to son Rocco and adopted baby David. Bet her kids are totally embarrassed about that *Sex* book, though.

2008

Hillary Rodham Clinton: In this year Hillary Clinton becomes the first woman to make a serious run for the American presidency, garnering eighteen million votes in the Democratic primary. Whatever one thinks of her politics, her mothering skills are hard to dispute: Look at how poised and lovely Chelsea turned out to be!